For Margaret

Be proud —

Love,

Bill Halloran
1988.

Proud To Be A Teacher

Proud to be a Teacher by Bill Halloran

READING, INC.
OREGON

First Reading, Inc. Edition, 1988
Copyright © 1988 by Bill Halloran
All rights reserved
Published in the United States by
Reading, Inc., Oregon City, Oregon
Library of Congress Catalog Card No.: 87-62845
ISBN 0-943867-00-2
Printed in the United States

For
Beth—My Daughter
Alice—My Mother
"Harp"—My Father
With Love

CONTENTS

Preface   8

PART ONE   **Looking Back**   11
               Second Grade Magic   13
               Phyllis   18
               Thanks, Miss Doyle, Wherever You Are   20
               Seven Bounces   29
               Smith and Wesson   34

PART TWO   **Classroom Years**   37
               Could Life Get Any Sweeter?   38
               Where Was the Chapter on Indoor Recess?   40
               Robins, Bluebirds and Vultures   45
               Please, Mr. Halloran, Just One More Chapter? 49
               No Principalship   56
               Robert   59
               Meeting the Authors   63

PART THREE **Traveling Teacher**   77
               An Invitation   78
               Marathon Week   80
               Cardboard Boxes   83
               Bill Martin Jr.   84
               Discovering the Power of Books   89
               Taking a Risk   92
               Shirley   100
               Another Survivor   104
               Burnout is Real   125
               My Prison Term   127
               The Women in My Life   130
               Stella   135

PART FOUR **Some Things To Think About**   151
               The Gray Group   152
               Building a Foundation   155
               Book Reports   158
               Fads in Education   162
               Surviving   171
               Rewards   176

PART FIVE **Looking Ahead**   187
               A Celebration   188
               Poem   192

Preface

During most of my teaching career, friends and colleagues have expected me to write a book—any kind of book. A few times I did try. Once I started a classroom idea book, but soon asked myself, "Does the world really need one more idea book?" Then I thought I would compile a book listing some of the best literature with accompanying synopses for kids. I thought such a book would be of great help to teachers and parents who wanted to select books that would capture kids and make them want to be life long readers. It was a good idea, and still is, but it has already been well done. So, that idea went into the waste basket along with all the others.

I really think my best idea was to write THE BILL HALLORAN HEALTH DITTO BOOK—Fill in the Blanks and You'll Never Pick Your Nose Again. The funny thing is my health book would have sold and probably would have made me a very wealthy man.

Then I remembered what Bill Martin Jr., a man who has made important and exciting contributions to language arts, said to me a very long time ago when I was discussing my dilemma with him. He said, "Don't try to force a book. You and you alone will know when you are ready." I'm glad I listened to Bill. Now, I am ready.

I have spent the last thirteen years traveling throughout the United States and parts of other countries talking about kids, books, and reading. Woven into each presentation have been stories from my teaching years in an elementary classroom along with some of my travel experiences. Because the stories always seemed to fit so naturally into my presentations, I did not realize their power and importance for a long while.

After being on the road for a couple of years, a strange thing happened. In most of my audiences throughout the country familiar faces started to appear. I found that many teachers and parents kept coming back to my presentations for a second, third, and even fourth time. Often they would ask me to tell a particular story again. I was flattered, of course, but confused and a little embarrassed by their presence. I asked myself, "What could these people be doing here again? Are they hiding out from their principals? Good grief! Are there such things as educational groupies?"

I remember how I used to intentionally leave out some of my stories so my talk would not be repetitious and dull for the people who had returned to hear me. Of course, I was completely disregarding the rest of my audience. My reward for such consideration was usually a reprimand in the form of, "You left out the story about _____ and the one about _____." From those who were there for the first time I heard, "I'm so disappointed. I came to hear you tell about _____. I want to hear you tell about _____. I need to hear you tell about _____."

Need was a strong word. Based on that word alone I decided to keep my stories in. New ones fell into place as I went along, and yet, I did not fully understand just what was happening. I watched and waited. The people kept coming – again and again.

I found out something very important through my stories; teachers want to know that you understand. They want to laugh with you, cry with you, think with you, and grow with you. They want to survive. That was really it. They needed help surviving on a day to day basis. Without knowing it, I was helping teachers to get through their day, hours – sometimes seconds. Besides, who can resist a good story?

So, after a great deal of thought, I decided to write a book about my own personal experiences as an educator and tell all those stories one more time. For all those who will find this book helpful, or at least enjoyable, you can thank the people who never let me leave out my stories.

In order to write the first draft of this book, I ran away to New York City and locked myself in a room at the Sheraton City Squire at 51st and 7th. I figured that at a room rate of $150.00 a day I'd be forced to finish in record time. I did finish the first draft, which led to the book you are now holding in your hands. My only hope, now, is that you will enjoy reading the account of my career as much as I enjoyed living it.

B.H.

Part One
Looking Back

Second Grade Magic

My story began many years ago. Walking home from second grade on that last day of school with my report card in hand, I was so happy that the long summer was ahead of me. Little did I realize that this joyous day would soon turn into tragedy—one that would have far-reaching effects upon my life and future career.

I handed my mother my report card, waiting anxiously for her to open and read it. Expecting smiles and happy words, I was stunned by what I heard. "You stayed back," she said softly. Those three words hit me with such thunderous force, that I can still remember the sudden shock. Even a seven year old knows the immediate implications, if not the far-reaching ones, of staying back no matter how gently the words are spoken. I remember, and I can feel the crush of those words for every child who has ever heard them or ever will.

All summer I dreaded that first day of school in the fall. I would be the dumb kid going back to second grade again, and everyone would know it. It was probably the only time in my life that I wanted to run away.

When that fatal first day of school arrived, I **was** the dumb kid, just as I had expected. I don't know how long I sat there in the heat of my embarrassment before an unexpected and wonderful thing happened. My mother appeared at the classroom door. She spoke to the teacher for a few minutes as I nervously tried to lip read their conversation. Then my mother walked in, took me out of that second grade, and brought me to St. Mary's School—to Sister Helen Elizabeth's second grade. My life was saved.

It was love at first sight. Sister Helen Elizabeth was

young and beautiful, and I knew she loved me at first sight, too. This was to be my first romantic encounter. I knew from the start it would be torrid. I must also tell you that the affair continues to this very day, only now we are the same age. Needless to say, I had a wonderful second year in second grade.

One thing I remember clearly about Sister Helen Elizabeth is that she would wink at me every day. I went to school some days just to get that wink. To this day I cannot wink, and I think it's Sister's fault. If I ever want to wink I have to hold one eyelid and use my other hand to flip my other lid up and down. I seldom ever try to wink, as I would probably get arrested.

So you see, my philosophy on report cards, retention, and home-school communication began forming very early in my life. I think one reason I was destined to become a teacher is so that I could help to prevent history from repeating itself. Sometimes I feel that it's a losing battle, but I continue to try. At the very least, I was able to make a difference with the kids who passed through my classroom.

Now don't get me wrong. I'm not against retention, but I'm against the way retention is handled. I'm against the negative attitude that usually exists among teachers and children toward retention. Before any child is retained, the child and the parents must be prepared. No surprises. The child's peers must be helped to understand, also. Of course, this kind of understanding must start at the very beginning of the school years and continue to the end.

Then there are other questions that could be raised. Would the child be successful with a different teacher? Is it that the child isn't ready to learn, or is it that the teacher isn't ready to teach the child? Who is responsible for the retained child—the new teacher or the retaining teacher? Are both teachers responsible for helping to make a second year at a grade level successful? If every measure isn't taken to insure that the child be immersed in an intellectually and emotionally nourishing environment, then the child in question could suffer long-range, if not permanent, damage. As educators, we must never forget that the child's self-image is so very important and so very fragile.

I, for one, have definitely experienced that feeling of self-doubt that accompanies low self-image. That's why it's amazing to me that I now have a career as an educator and a speaker. I must have subconsciously done so just to prove that mountains can be climbed, barriers can be knocked down, and ambitions can be achieved in spite of a variety of obstacles.

When I was a young boy I stuttered. For a child, there isn't much that is more frustrating than not being able to express yourself—to actually get the words out. You feel like you're going to explode and, at the same time, afraid you won't. During my stuttering years there was no help for kids with speech problems. You sat in your seat praying that the teacher wouldn't call on you. Of course, your prayers were not always answered.

At first the other kids laughed at the stuttering, but the laughter soon turned to annoyance and anger. The kids had no patience. They didn't want to hear the stuttering anymore. I remember the moans all around me when I was called on. Even the teacher became weary of my stuttering and eventually did not call on me at all. Although I was relieved to be left alone, it also meant a kind of hopeless abandonment.

Understandably, I would never volunteer for anything. Soon I became labeled a non-reader and a slow student. No one in my life realized that there was nothing wrong with my intellect or my desire to learn.

I really don't know how I overcame my stuttering. I only remember my mother being very patient with me, always taking time to listen no matter how long it took me to get the words out. She never looked away and never pretended to listen.

Every day I stand up to give a speech I think, "What a wonderful thing to be able to address hundreds, sometimes thousands of people at one time. I'm a speaker!" I really did climb what was a high mountain for me. I must admit, though, that there are a few loose rocks on the mountaintop. As much as I enjoy listening to Mel Tillis sing, I am very careful never to listen to him speak if I am soon to give a presentation. I know I'll never stutter again, but it does give me an uneasy feeling to hear someone else struggle to speak.

The school years passed, and there was not another Sister Helen Elizabeth nor another magical year. I feel sad about that because every teacher and every year should have at least some magical qualities. That's a big part of teaching, making our subject matter come alive, so that our kids will love learning and beg for more.

Most of my time these days is spent in wanting to be that special magical teacher and looking for other teachers who have the same desire. The age of my students is unimportant, for people never lose their need for recognition, warmth, encouragement, respect, and knowledge. Today, more than any other time in education, we need the magic in our classrooms. We are losing so many kids to the streets, to the world of continuous day dreams, and, sadly enough, to suicide.

My high school days were ordinary. I signed up for the business courses knowing there would be no college in my future. After four years of shorthand, book-keeping, typing, etc., graduation day arrived and I was ready to face the world.

At eighteen I entered the business world. I got a job in the local bicycle factory, Columbia Manufacturing. Ironically, Columbia also made school desks and chairs. I began my career sweeping floors, loading cold boxcars in winter, and working in the heat of the bonderizing room in the summer.

It was also that summer that I met Phyllis. Because of that meeting, my life would take an unexpected turn, although it would take a few years for the wheels to be redirected.

Phyllis

One hot summer night, as was the custom, a group of us went up to the girl scout camp and tried to be cool with the counselors. Well, it so happened that Phyllis was one of the counselors. As I recall, there was hardly time for a quick hello and the exchange of a few words, never mind time for being cool. Strangely enough, our paths did not cross again for about two years, but we found out later that we both had done a lot of thinking about each other, even after such a brief and awkward first meeting.

My life at the factory continued uneventfully. It wasn't a bad job, but it wasn't great either. It gave me a decent pay check, some benefits, and a three to six week layoff in the winter, which I fully enjoyed. It was all I knew. What else could there be?

Then one night my phone rang. It was Phyllis on the other end of the line. She was now a junior in college and was going to be staying at her girlfriend's for a semester— right next door to where I lived. I was surprised enough to hear her voice after two years, but you can imagine my shock when she asked me if we might get together. Phyllis was into liberation long before the movement began.

Foolishly, as I was trying to deal with the surprise of it all, I said I was busy. I still can't believe I said that. Five minutes later I called her back and said I was free after all. Well, what would you have done?! The evening turned out to be great, so great we spent every night after that together. Neither one of us was on a very big "expense account", but, true to form, the long walks, endless conversations, movies, and an occasional splurge on a dinner was more than we required. We were in love, and we knew almost immediately that we would someday marry.

Again, and in the middle of the greatest love affair of all

time, my life took an unavoidable twist. My best friend had talked me into signing up for the draft. You've got it! The minute the word reached Washington that I had a good reason to stay home, I got my orders. So, I went off to serve my country for two years. Wasn't that great timing?

Actually, it all turned out just fine. Phyllis finished college and got her first teaching job. I spent most of my two years as a radio operator in Japan. As promised, I returned from the communications war and Phyllis and I took up where we had left off.

Picking Phyllis up after school was almost as much a challenge as boot camp had been. First her kids would announce, "Your father is here." This didn't help, in view of the fact that my hair was already prematurely half gray. Then I'd have to literally wrestle her away from some ardent and very protective first graders. I don't think the kids ever fully trusted me with their teacher, but they did all come to our wedding in the spring of 1958. Now I can understand their reluctance at having their magical year interrupted. There were a few hold-outs who refused to call her by her new name when she returned to school.

The following fall we settled in Westfield, Massachusetts, a small town in the western part of the state. I went back to the factory, and Phyllis continued to teach. Our daughter, Lizbeth, otherwise known as Beth, was born in the fall of 1959. Life couldn't have been better—or so I thought.

Phyllis wanted me to go to college. I kept asking her and myself just what my going to college could give us that we didn't already have. According to Phyllis, my favorite and most foolish response at the end of a discussion on my going to school was, "Besides, I like making bicycles."

Thanks, Miss Doyle, Wherever You Are

The years began to pass, and I was not a kid anymore. Thirty was getting closer and closer. Phyllis kept telling me that I was wasting my talent, and that I was denying my intelligence. I had never heard words like that before, so it took a while for me to accept them.

Finally, I weakened. I signed up for two evening courses at Holyoke Community College. I took a modern math course, which I didn't understand, and an English composition course which was all Greek to me. Why I ever stayed with the English composition course I'll never know. That class was sheer torture. I didn't know a noun from a verb or a period from a comma. I'm exaggerating a little here, but my English background needed much refreshing, and there I was in a composition course with Miss Doyle from Smith College. Fortunately for me, Miss Doyle was teaching an evening course at Holyoke Community College, and I landed in her class.

Every week we had to write a composition, and every week Miss Doyle asked me to stay after the others had gone. Soon she didn't have to ask—I just knew to stay. With great kindness she would always tell me that I would have to do something about my writing skills. She would say that I never use commas and seldom put periods in the right places. I was encouraged to use capital letters now and then, and I was told that my writing style was run-on. I was delighted to have any style at all! But no matter how bad it got, Miss Doyle always added that I had wonderful ideas. I think after sixteen weeks I probably drove her to drink, while she drove me to keep trying.

On the last night of the course a strange thing happened. After the final exam she asked me to stay after— as usual. Holding my exam in her hand she said that she wasn't even going to correct it. She said she already knew that I probably barely passed the exam, but that she was going to give me a "C" for the course. Then she spoke words that have never left me. "I may never see you again," she began, "but I know you are going to make your mark in this world, probably in the area of writing, or literature, or something related. I'm not quite sure of just what you will do, but someday you will be known." She smiled, shook her head very slightly, probably in dismay at having survived me week after torturous week, and then walked down the hall. I never did see her again.

I did make my mark in the area of children's literature, Miss Doyle. You were close. Once again, a little magic entered my life. It had been a long time since second grade and Sister Helen Elizabeth.

Thank you, Miss Doyle.

The next step was to take the entrance exam at Westfield State College. After the exam, the dean called me into his office, handed me a book, told me to study hard, and to try the exam again in six months. He never came right out and said that I had failed. He didn't have to.

I thought I was home free. I had failed the entrance exam, and that was that. There would be no college for me. I simply wasn't college material. I should have known that Phyllis wouldn't give up that easily. I studied that book for six months. Exam time rolled around, and, once more, the dean called me into his office. This strongly principled man smiled at me and said that I was going to be a freshman in the fall. He never did give me my marks. All I know is that he helped and guided another person. That is a very important part of being an educator. I wish there were a way around the marking system. I'm sure there were thousands of people who achieved great things in their lifetimes in spite of poor grades. When grades are the only measure of a person, deeply hidden talents and self-confidence can remain unrecognized, preventing people from realizing meaningful accomplishments, not to mention day-to-day contentment.

I was so busy trying to get into college that I never gave a thought to where I would get the money to pay for my first semester. It just so happened that Phyllis' parents, two wonderfully supportive people, gave me the $100.00 (Can you believe a semester for $100.00?) I needed. Sam and Lena knew that I was trying to do something for my family, as much as for myself, and they always did what they could whenever they could. I started going to Westfield State part time, but because of their continuous encouragement and financial help I was eventually able to go full time. I shall always be grateful to them. I do regret that Sam did not live long enough to see how far that initial $100.00 took me.

My first semester in college was a complete disaster. I couldn't pass anything, and I was working like I had never worked before. When people come to hear me speak, I think they suspect that I was born with a silver microphone in front of me. I am often asked if I have ever gone to acting classes, drama school, or had special training on my way to becoming a speaker. Very few people realize the road I had to take to reach this point in my career.

At the end of the first semester, I had made up my mind to leave college and go back to the factory. After all, I had worked at that factory for thirteen years. My friends were there, and, more importantly, I wouldn't have to study. The work was easier and the hours were shorter. I never realized how hard getting an education would be. The factory really looked better than ever to me.

Now all I had to do was break the news to Phyllis. That wouldn't be easy. Timing was everything. We were at the dentist's office—it was my turn in the chair—and when I came out and she was on her way in, I told her that I was leaving school. I hoped that the pain of the drill would hurt her more than the pain of my giving up. Phyllis said one thing as we drove home that day; "If you stay in school one full year and then you still want to leave, I'll never say another word, and you can do anything you want."

By the end of that first year I was determined to stay and get my degree—even if it killed me. It almost did. In all honesty, I did catch on and really enjoyed the challenge of accomplishment. I even made the dean's list my junior and senior years.

In spite of my accomplishments, my college years were not the carefree, fun-filled years they are for many students. My days were filled with endless hours of study. I worked the night shift at the factory and held down additional part-time jobs, while trying to be a good husband and father. Phyllis taught all those years, even in the summer. She spent every night helping me with my studies and watching over my commas and periods. Through it all, she managed to be the best possible mother to Beth.

The strange part of it all was that I was determined to get a degree, but I really didn't want to be a teacher. That changed during my junior year. The first day I walked into that fifth grade to do my practice teaching I knew I was in the right place. To this day I feel that my road was paved from the very beginning, that I was meant to be a teacher. All I had to do was follow the road.

My senior year was wonderful. Not only did I accept the Outstanding Student Teacher Award, but I knew my life would never be the same again. It wasn't the award that gave me so much satisfaction, rather that I was finally a teacher, or so I thought. I was about to enter a special new world. Today, twenty some odd years later, that world is still very special to me.

Sometimes I think of those days of struggle, and it still strikes me as strange that studies, term papers, and exams were so difficult, and teaching is so easy. I wonder if, under the present system, they actually have a lot to do with each other.

1. Sixth Grade

2. High School (Classroom sign is on Bill's desk).

3. U.S. Army—Fort Dix

4. April 19,1958—"I did."

5. June 1966—Graduation Day

Seven Bounces

Before I leave my college years and venture with you out into the world, I must mention four of my professors who helped me to become the teacher I am today—the four who helped form my philosophy.

I was planning my courses for my junior year, and I was told a wonderful woman was going to teach a course in children's literature. It was being offered as an elective. In those days I thought if you had seen one kid's book you had seen them all. I really didn't want to take a course in children's literature, but when it came down to the wire, I had to make a choice between children's literature and chemistry. Well, which one would you have chosen?

Barbara Pilon walked into the class that first day, and she began reading a picture book to us. She showed us some of the most wonderful kid's books. I knew immediately that a whole new world was opening up to me. After that first class I got into my car and drove to Johnson's Book Store in Springfield, Massachusetts and purchased Maurice Sendak's *Where the Wild Things are*. This wonderful book still sits in our collection and is still used.

I couldn't wait for Dr. Pilon's class. Children's books were absolutely magical for me, and I couldn't get enough of them. I started to buy my own books. There was a real drive in me to have those jewels at my fingertips. Phyllis shared my enthusiasm, and we went happily on our way spending money that shouldn't have been spent on books. That book buying drive has never left us. Many years have passed, and our collection of children's books is one of the largest and most exciting private collections in the country.

Thank you, Barbara Pilon.

I must mention Dr. Don Landry, because he brought excitement and enthusiasm to his teaching of the language arts. It was wonderful to go to his classes, because he loved and believed in what he was teaching. So many teachers go through the motions, bored with the whole business. Don Landry's excitement flowed to his students naturally as he challenged their imaginations. I knew right away that the flow of energy and enthusiasm would be a major part of my teaching. The cycle has to be started by the teacher.

Thank you, Don Landry.

Dr. Paul Bogan, who taught physical education, made me aware of other ingredients for success in teaching. He taught patience, understanding, and having time for all of his students. He taught me this through his own teaching style. These qualities are among the most important for a teacher to possess.

Thank you, Paul Bogan.

And then there was John O'Shea who taught geography. Lord, I didn't want to take geography. I just wanted to get my degree and get a job, but you have to play the game. No geography, no degree. Phyllis said, "He's Irish; you're Irish. Just to make sure, sign in as Bill O'Halloran." Not Bad! I thought it just might work. It didn't! John O'Shea wasn't the least bit impressed with our shared ethnic background, in spite of the fact that he was, and still is, as Irish as they come. So I was stuck with a semester of geography— with participation expected.

The first week the hat was passed with those damn term paper topics. You put your hand in the hat and pulled your twenty-four-hour companion topic. I wasn't looking forward to the hours of research that were ahead of me. I must admit that Phyllis did help a lot with gathering information for me. She did all the typing, too. I know that sounds unfair, but we were both desperate for me to get a degree, so we worked at it together.

Well, I put my hand in the hat and prayed to God that Phyllis would get a good topic. Times were getting tough and she was beginning to show signs of rebellion. I pulled out a slip of folded paper and held my breath. Carefully, I unfolded it and read the one word that appeared: CRANBERRIES. Cranberries! Hell, I had to write a paper on cranberries. Rather, Phyllis had to write a paper on cranberries!

I broke the news to Phyllis that night at dinner, and she said, "No, no, no! There is a limit, and this is it. YOU can research cranberries, because I quit."! I tried to explain that I had so much other work to do plus two jobs and no knowledge of cranberries. There was no compassion in her eyes when she looked at me and flippantly said, "Look on the Ocean Spray can."

When I heard the name Ocean Spray a light went on. The Ocean Spray Cranberry Company was located just down the road a few miles on Cape Cod, Massachusetts. I sat right down and wrote a letter to the Company telling them of my predicament. Guess what? Ocean Spray did my term paper! I was so happy! I received enough information on cranberries to do a couple of good papers. Right or wrong, please don't pass judgment. I was a desperate aging man. I did a little paraphrasing, changed their cover for mine, and turned in my paper to John O'Shea. I got an A. Rather, Ocean Spray got an A. Please, when you go grocery shopping, buy Ocean Spray products. After all, how many big outfits do you know that would help a poor guy with a term paper? Isn't it funny how what seems almost like nonsense years later was life sustaining at one time? Isn't some of the stuff you remember about your education funny, too?

I must admit that I learned some interesting facts while doing that paper. For example, there were hundreds of people standing at a conveyor belt with all the cranberries passing by on the belt. Each person would pick up one cranberry at a time and bounce that berry seven times. If the berry didn't bounce seven times it was a bad berry and was put in the bad pile. If it bounced seven times it was a good berry and was put in the good pile. Can you believe it? Phyllis suggested that if I didn't get my degree I could always be a cranberry bouncer!

The last day of the course arrived, which meant a final exam. I felt as though I couldn't possibly be tested, because I didn't know enough to be tested on. That was the general feeling experienced by most of the "older students". I mentioned, in my worried state, that I might have to take geography over. Phyllis gave a reply that was to the point and left no room for misunderstanding. She said that I had better pass the exam, or I'd be on my own the next time around. Do you have any idea of how much I hoped that I'd see a few questions on cranberries? I hoped in vain.

I'll never forget the morning of that exam. John O'Shea walked in carrying the tests. I think he knew some of us were a little tense. He set the tests on his desk, looked at us for a few moments, then said, "This course, this test, this final grade has little to do with your life or your happiness." I thought, "That's what you think." He continued, "You are on your own roads. Take from me what you can and continue along those roads. I did not come here to fail you. I came to give to you. Now, take from me what is most valuable in aiding you in future success and happiness. Take what you can and move on. Oh, there's one more thing; If you don't know the answer to a question, just write in the word alfalfa, and I'll mark it correct." Praise the Lord!! I had a chance!

The exam began. I began the exam, and I answered the first question. Seven bounces. No, just a little humor. When I finally did get stuck on a question, John O'Shea was walking around the room and must have noticed that I was in trouble. He walked over to me, put his arm on my shoulder and said, "What's the matter, Bill?" I replied, "I don't know how to spell alfalfa." Well, he started to laugh and said, "You've missed the point. Write in anything and go down your road. Live your life to the fullest. This test means nothing."

I think of John O'Shea and all that I did learn from him—not just about geography, but about life, teaching, and human emotions. He modeled for his students the kind of teacher that should touch everyone's life at least once, for he made a positive difference. I have never forgotten about the road, marks, and giving. I never will. I have done my best to pass it on.

Thank you, John O'Shea.

Smith and Wesson

Now to find a job. I looked forward to the search as I began making appointments for interviews with prospective school systems. It wasn't easy. I was really surprised and disappointed at some of the strange questions I was asked. Some of the people interviewing me were a bit strange, too, as I recall. I remember thinking, "Is this what I worked so hard for all these years?"

Looking back, most of it was rather humorous. I never admitted to not knowing the answer to a question. After all, I was supposed to be an expert, an expert in spite of never having had a classroom of my own. As I recall, some of the interviews went something like this:

Q.   Mr. Halloran, what is your favorite reading series?

A.   Smith and Wesson. (I had only seen one reading series in practice teaching. What did I know? I actually remember one interviewer asking me if Smith and Wesson were a good system. He didn't know much either. I said it was a dynamite system. He wrote it down! I scratched him off my list.).

Q.   Mr. Halloran, can you teach math?

A.   Trig's my hobby.

Q.   Mr. Halloran, can you teach art?

A.   I paint ceilings in the summer.

I finally landed a job in a sixth grade classroom. It's funny how I accepted the job offer from the one system I was really not interested in because it was quite a distance from my home. The interviewer, Carl Tripp, was so intelligent and aware of the educational scene, that I knew I wanted to work with someone like him. He became my principal.

Well, there I was—a teacher. I had my own classroom, and I was bursting at the seams. It truly was a glorious time in my life. I just knew that I was going to be the very best elementary teacher in the system, the state, the country! That was my goal.

Part Two
Classroom Years

Could Life Get Any Sweeter?

My elementary classroom teaching career began at a school in Longmeadow, a town about forty minutes from my home. I always enjoyed the ride to and from school, because it gave me time to clear my mind and get centered, in spite of the fast pace of the highways I traveled. Greenwood Park was a brand new school about to open its doors in September of 1966. It was **my** brand new school, and I took great joy in going into **my** classroom throughout the summer months, as I prepared to launch **my** career. I was to be the only male teacher in the building, which allowed me to have a private john. **My** school, **my** classroom, **my** john. Could life get any sweeter? Little did I know that women's liberation would soon be on my heels each time I entered what became **our** john. I must admit that it took a little getting used to. It also made life interesting.

I wanted everything to be just right on the first day of school, so I took many trips to that new classroom during the summer months. Sometimes I just sat at my desk thinking. Other times I took great delight in going through all those new untouched supplies. The "my" list was growing; now I had **my** supplies.

Soon enough, the power of my material possessions let go of me, and I realized that the most important ingredient was missing. I can still remember my eagerness to meet the kids. I'm sure every first year teacher can still remember the same feelings I'm describing. I was ready, able, and fearless! Bring on **my** kids.

I was not disappointed on that first day of school, nor any day after. Of course, there were highs and lows, but I was excited about teaching, and my excitement flowed to the kids. Their excitement flowed right back to me. It dawned on me during that unforgettable year, that teaching is like a circle. How simple. Whenever I hear Harry Chapin's *All My Life's a Circle*, I quietly remember that wonderful awareness that came to me so early in my career. It's still with me.

Where Was the Chapter on Indoor Recess?

The days were filled with wonderful new experiences and challenges. I don't think I ever worked so hard in my life to keep up with everything. I was amazed at what I was learning. But somebody definitely left out a few things in college. As I think back, seldom, if ever, did anyone ever really talk about kids. We were immersed in content and writing those damn lesson plans until three in the morning.

Is it possible that many of the people teaching prospective teachers never had much to do with children on a continuous basis? For example, who ever mentioned recess? More importantly, where was the chapter in the textbooks on **indoor** recess? If you have ever had the experience of indoor recess, you know exactly what I mean. At one point, I seriously entertained the thought of heading a lobby against this inhuman duty. Like this teacher, there are thousands of long-suffering teachers who would like to see indoor recess declared illegal. I made my kids go out even if it were fifty degrees below zero with an accompanying blizzard. "I'll stand here in the hall and watch kids." If you think I'm being just a little too hard on the subject, stop and think. Think back to that first indoor recess, the one that hit you like a sledgehammer, the one that came when you had one foot out the door pointed toward the teacher's room—and that was just the beginning of fifteen minutes of shock, dismay and self-doubt. Think back. You'll know what I mean.

Classroom parties. Now there's a subject that needs a

little attention at the undergraduate level. I couldn't wait for the first Halloween party. I was like a kid myself. After the first cupcake whizzed across the room I thought, "Who needs this? What IS this?" My final word on how to deal with classroom parties, if really forced into them, is call in sick. This goes for birthday parties, too. Just tell the kids they won't be getting a year older until they move on to the next grade.

There's one other little delicate matter that should get a little attention before one innocently closes the classroom door. Why don't kids know about deodorant? After a day with twenty-five or thirty ten and eleven year old kids you start to feel as though you've been gassed. I believe teachers should be provided with gas insurance— both kinds! And if you don't know what I'm talking about, you haven't really been there. Some days it's so bad there's a green haze hanging over the room. There's no staying "on task" when you're choking to death. Like when you're in a reading group and suddenly it hits! You try not to breathe because you'll die on the spot. Then the little kid next to you looks up and says, "I didn't do that." Some days the kids try to blame you. Some days they're right.

And those magical magic markers! I had six dozen of the most beautiful magic markers on that first day. I had every color under the rainbow. I loved my magic markers. Then the kids came. I never knew that kids don't put the caps back on when they're through with them. In one week I had six dozen of the most beautiful dry magic markers in the whole world. I went to my principal to ask for more. He just laughed!

Ah, yes. Evaluations. We had three formal observations followed by a conference each year. Do you remember your first observation? My principal would always say he'd be in sometime during the month!!

Hell, that meant I had to have a month of outstanding lessons. I would be exhausted or dead in a month. That first year I had a month of dynamic lessons, and on the last day of the month when I was nearly dead, I met Carl in the hall. He said, "I didn't get to you this month, Bill. I'll be in sometime next month." They took me to the nearest hospital. Now, you know what happens after several months of high anxiety—you finally sit back and relax a little, even take it a little easy. That's when the door opens and in he walks!

When I was finally observed for the first time, it was a complete disaster. Of all things, I was teaching the seven rules of the comma. Anyone who really knows me knows how I feel about commas. Now you will understand why I feel the way I do. Just how dynamic can you make seven comma rules, I ask you? Well, when Carl started to write in his notebook, I got nervous. I not only did the seven comma rules, but I also did nouns, verbs, adjectives, and prepositions all in twenty minutes. I think if he hadn't left after twenty minutes I would have finished the whole book of punctuation and grammar. The poor kids—their heads were spinning. I told them not to worry, that we'd have a review the next day!

At the end of the day I heard on the intercom, "Mr. Halloran, will you please stop by my office for a few minutes before you go home?" I knew what it felt like to be a kid on his way to the principal's office. Now, if you were called to the office, and you were not told to close the door you were home free. If you were told to close the door, you were in for it. That day I didn't even wait for the instructions. I closed the door and sat down. He said, "Bill, don't you think you covered just a little bit too much material in twenty minutes?" I said, "You made me nervous." Then he said, "Bill, I'm the one who hired you. I'm rooting for you. I want you to be the best. Relax and do your teaching." I remember thinking, "Why the hell didn't you tell me that when you came in?"

I think a few words on parent conferences are in order, too, since no one had ever metioned those either. My first one was a disaster. I almost got arrested. The conference started out really great. I was prepared and the mother was lovely. She asked intelligent questions, and I gave brilliant answers. Before I knew it, the conference was just about over. That's when it happened. This pleasant woman, obviously satisfied with the meeting, started to put on her coat. Something got stuck down her back. She asked me if I would help, so I put my arm down her back and tried to unhook whatever was caught. At that point my sleeve button got caught on something down there, and when I started to pull she started to yell. The more I pulled the more she yelled. I never did find my button, and, thank heaven, I never saw the woman again. My principal later told me to stick to the conference and never mind helping women in distress. Today I'd be serving ten to life for such a display of naiveté.

Did someone just mention field trips? Again, I must pause and wonder why no one had ever mentioned field trips. Why hadn't someone prepared me? Why didn't someone stop me? I was allowed to take my class on a bus to New York City. Can you believe it? New York City! I was going to give my kids an experiential background whenever possible. I was going to show my kids the "Big Apple." Let me tell you—they showed me the "Big Apple"!! I have to laugh when I stop to think of how I must have looked to anyone who might have taken notice of me. I think "madman" would say it all. To this day I am impressed with the energy and enthusiasm I had, not to mention my idiocy when I decided to take the kids for a ride on the Statton Island Ferry. Think of it—three dozen kids on a boat in New York Harbor. We almost lost three in the bay that day.

Do you want to know where I took my class the next year? Down the hall to the boiler room. I opened the door and said, "There's the furnace—now get back to the room." The kids asked, "Is that the field trip?" I said, "You've got it. Draw it."

I don't know what made me think kids only got sick at home. Perhaps, because I have such a weak stomach, I just wouldn't allow it any other way. Boy, was I wrong. Kids do get sick in school, and my list of things never mentioned in college grew a little longer. The first time one of my sixth graders heaved in the classroom I did too! The kid was in the corner heaving, and I was in the sink. Some of the kids ran to get the principal. In he came. With the sound of disbelief in his voice, he said, "Bill, you can't do that!" I, with the sound of total abandon in my voice, said, "You just watch me! And get that kid out of here!"

In spite of all the things I had to learn along the way, I was determined to keep my teaching and my classroom alive and exciting. I knew I wouldn't be able to stand the boredom that creeps into many classrooms, and, if I wouldn't be able to stand it, my kids wouldn't either. Right away I knew that it was my job to keep everything going. My own enthusiasm was my finest teaching tool. It still is to this very day. I discovered that it would not be the bulletin boards, the equipment, the gimmicks, or even the books that would motivate most of my kids. It would be me. I would be the initial source of enthusiasm that would flow to the kids and then back to me. When kids are all grown up they don't look back and say, "I loved my sixth grade projector." If they do, you were the pits. If you did your job, the kids will look back and say, "I loved my sixth grade teacher," or, more importantly, "I loved my sixth grade year."

Robins, Bluebirds and Vultures

I was never satisfied with the reading program. I had my three groups, because it was expected. That was the way it was done. I had my robins, bluebirds, and vultures, but it all seemed so flat and dull. I often wondered if anybody was really learning anything and liking it.

Then one day the proverbial straw landed. We were reading the basal reader story *Sound of Summer Running,* a story about a pair of sneakers that ran through the summer having a wonderful time. Well, I did everything I could to make that story as interesting as it could be. I even brought in a huge pair of smelly sneakers. I really did! We read the story, and then I started my questioning. One little boy raised his hand and said, "Mr. Halloran, this really stinks." He wasn't referring to the sneakers. I looked at him for a moment and said, "You're right. It does stink. Close your books, kids, and we'll do something else." I knew then and there that reading had to be better than that. I was determined to make it better.

I am still amazed that I didn't know enough to read to my sixth graders right from the start. All those reading courses, all those hours of preparation in college had been geared to teaching skills, and no one ever talked about the most important element of the program—reading to kids. There is a never ending need to read out loud, and it is still sitting on the back burner in most schools. Reading to kids exposes them to the world of reading in the most personal of ways, and they can't fail. The rewards of reading to kids are great. First, and most importantly, the kids learn to like reading painlessly. They quickly start to look forward to the wonderful stories connected to the printed word. Whether for five minutes or for fifty, the teacher and the kids are bonded. It's as enjoyable for the teacher as it is for the kids—maybe even more so.

Why is it so difficult to get so many educators to understand and believe that reading to kids is not a time filler? Rather, it is the fastest way to get kids to want to read—to develop vocabulary, oral expression, and to think. If kids can hear the words and bring to those words their own set of experiences, then they are on the road to reading—the kind of reading that will last a lifetime. It's common sense. Why does everything have to be profound and earth shaking before we accept it? We don't have to buy a kit, a special set of materials, a book of instructions, hardware, software, etc. All we have to do is go to the library. After affecting a positive attitude toward reading, we must then immerse our kids in books of all sizes, shapes, colors and content, so that they will experience the best addiction of their lives.

Do you know that in most schools we stop reading to our kids somewhere around second or third grade? I even heard kindergarten and first grade teachers say that they don't have time. Let's be honest. If we understand and believe in reading to children, we will make the time for it, or fight for the time. We must stop and take a good long hard look at the way we are "skilling" our kids into a hatred of reading and a misunderstanding of books. Skills are a sensible and necessary aid to the reading process, but in many schools there is no balance. Our kids are buried under a mound of isolated skills lessons from the first grade on, sometimes earlier, with no picture books and novels to counterbalance. The reading program that focuses mainly on skills lessons and skills sheets is doomed from the start. Such a program will never create contented lifelong readers. Scores might go up, temporarily, but are the kids reading and begging for more? If we continue to blindly send our kids into the world with hundreds of isolated skills, even the hard work that goes into the teaching of skills will be for nothing. We will have created, yet, another generation of nonreaders.

I've said it thousands of times already, and I'll say it thousands of times more—the joy and excitement of reading must come from the teacher in school after the parents have set the scene at home. Even if the parents have never read to their children, it's not too late to start in school. Maybe we would be better off if we tried to help parents to understand the importance of reading to children, instead of sending home extra mimeographed skills sheets to be done.

There are dozens of writing programs on the market today and even more writing workshops and courses than ever before. I have heard more people out of education talk about reading being the first step to writing than the people in education. Listen to the successful writers talk about what contributed to their success. They almost always describe a parent, grandparent, or someone who read to them, who started them on a lifelong journey with books. A read-aloud program prepares the kids to write. It opens doors to worlds of fact and fiction, fantasy and reality, thoughts and words. What an easy and enjoyable way to start a reading/writing program. Think about it.

I am happy to say that more and more people are beginning to talk about reading to kids. Fifteen years ago there weren't too many educators promoting read-aloud. For my first few years in the consulting world I was not allowed to use the word literature in my program title or description. Imagine! The rationale was that teachers would not come for literature. Maybe they were right. I remember the day a very enthusias-

tic teacher came into my workshop room before I
started speaking. She looked at all the books on the
table with great enjoyment. Suddenly, she called to a
friend who was just coming into the room, "Come here
and look at all these wonderful books. I thought this
was supposed to be a reading workshop!"

We have made some progress but not enough. We need
to go further. We need to get the entire educational
community involved in promoting reading to kids in
our classrooms. We need to teach in an atmosphere
that allows us to read to our kids without feeling
guilty. We need to be part of a community that de-
mands that we have a read-aloud program going at
all times. We need to make the reading/writing connection. We need to make sure that we read to junior high
and high school kids. We need to understand and plan
a sequential read-aloud program that will be looked
upon as essential to good education as is math, science,
history and those never ending reading skills.

Please, Mr. Halloran, Just One More Chapter?

A successful read-aloud program is never hit or miss. It must be carefully planned without long intervals between books. There is little chance of forgetting to read once the teacher has started the program. The kids won't let a day pass without a few more pages, a few more chapters of the current book. The fastest way to quiet down a noisy class or breathe life back into a fast failing moment is to pick up the book you are currently reading. And remember to include picture books, novels, joke books, poetry, etc. Kids, like adults, enjoy variety.

Many teachers ask me for a read-aloud book. I can't give them one because it is a personal thing. Yes, there are many wonderful books I could recommend, but it's best for each person to have a strong feeling for the books to be chosen. You must be allowed to choose from a wide selection and not be boxed in by someone else's list of books that isn't right for you or your kids. It's important to look carefully at your program and possibly revise it yearly because each class has its own set of interests and needs. You must also be ready to make some unscheduled detours in mid road if your choices are not working.

Begin your read-aloud program the first day of the school year and take it right to the very last day. At first it might not be an easy program to put together, especially if you do not have adequate knowledge of children's literature. Start slowly. Start acquainting yourself with the library, spending a little time going through the shelves. You'll be amazed at how quickly you'll get caught up in the books. If your first choice doesn't work out, make another and another, if necessary. You'll hit your stride, and it will feel great. By the way, summer is a good time to do some searching, reading, and choosing. It's a good time to plan the beginning of your program, at least. Once you start reading to your kids you will know instinctively which book to choose when a new one is needed. You might want a book with a contrasting mood, or you might feel the need to read several books written by one author. You will know. Trust me!

You and your kids will have unforgettable experiences if you are willing to extend many of the books to related activities in the different subject areas. Each book has a natural connection to many of the disciplines, such as letter writing. After reading a particularly engrossing book or the books of a particular author, the natural next step is to write to the author. You'll find letter writing less painful than if you have the kids write to an imaginary person for no good reason.

Get the notion out of your heads that picture books are only for the primary grade kids. By doing an author study of Eric Carle, you will discover the tissue paper collage method he employs, and then you and your kids can try it in an art lesson. Another step would be to discover all the other illustrators who use the collage method and to compare the likenesses and differences among them. And, once more, you could write to the authors. Another outgrowth from Eric Carle could be looking into wordless books after reading *I see a Song*. That would be quite an interesting adventure because most teachers aren't even aware of the humor and sophistication to be found in the wordless books. It just goes on and on. One thing leads to another. The more you do the more there will be to do. For those of you who are thinking that you don't need one more thing to do, think again. The more you do along the lines I have suggested, the more you and your kids will enjoy learning. Again, trust me!

It's a little strange in a way, but I believe I have my job and position in this country in the area of literature and reading because I brought so much joy and excitement to my kids through my reading program by reading out loud every day. I exposed the kids to all kinds of books from the picture book to the novel. I worked hard to remove the stigma attached to some books, such as the picture books for the older students. There are just too many ways to look at a book to allow the attitude to prevail that picture books are for little kids. The creativity of the text, illustrations, or format of picture books alone makes them appropriate and necessary for all age groups.

It wasn't long before I became known as the man who could get kids to read. In truth, I wasn't able to get all my kids to read, but I was able to capture the majority of kids who had been turned off or had never been turned on to reading.

Let me go back to my first year of teaching and tell how reading out loud happened for me. I had a sixth grade class, and I knew nothing about reading to kids. Now, when I think back, it angers me. I had all those reading courses but didn't even know how important it was to read to kids across the grade levels, especially those who had been turned off for years through torturous skills lessons and dull reading material. It all happened quite by accident. They say that if you will listen to the kids they'll tell you exactly what they need. Thank heaven I was listening this time.

One day, about three months into the year, a boy walked up to me and handed me a book. He told me his aunt had given the book to him for his birthday and would I read a chapter to the class. I was not about to read to big kids. They should be doing the reading. Right? But the boy seemed so anxious to have me read, that I decided that a few minutes wouldn't hurt. The book happened to be *Charlie and the Chocolate Factory* by Roald Dahl. I realize that many people don't like this book, but for me it opened a wonderful door which I never closed again.

I began to read. Chapter one—Here Comes Charlie. When I finished reading I got quite a surprise because the kids started begging for more. Chapter two—Mr. Willy Wonka's Factory. And then, well, you've probably guessed what happened. Chapter three—.

I'll never forget how I read three chapters that day, and then we went on with the work of the day. The next morning the first words out of the mouths of most of the kids were, "Are you going to read about Charlie?" How amazing it was to me. These big kids loved hearing this little fantasy about a boy and a chocolate factory. The biggest surprise of all was that I, too, enjoyed the story and, most of all, I loved reading it out loud. My read-aloud program began as simply and as easily as that. The kids spoke and I listened. That day I learned something I should have known. Even though I had a very good literature course in college, reading to my kids on a daily basis never entered my mind.

Every day after that the kids begged me to read to them. They didn't have to beg too hard or too long. Nearing the end of *Charlie*, I began to panic. We didn't want it to end. I didn't stop worrying long enough to think of how easy it would be to just go and get another book to read. Luckily, as I was in the library desperately searching for just the right follow up book, I stumbled across *James and the Giant Peach*, also by Roald Dahl. I was so panicky over *Charlie* coming to an end, that I completely overlooked searching for another Dahl book. See what I mean about common sense being so important? *James* was perfect. It's the story of a huge marvelous peach that sails across the country and ends up in Central Park in New York City. What joy! They loved it.

When I finished reading *James*, I told the kids that I was going into New York for the weekend, and that I'd go to Central Park Saturday and look for the peach. Immediately, I received a roomful of moans and groans which quickly turned to, "Yea, Mr. Halloran. Go ahead. Do it, do it!" I thought, "I'll fix their wagons." I came in on Monday morning and said, "Kids, listen to me. I spent Saturday in Central Park, and I found it. I found the peach." More moans and groans came forth with a few boos for flavor. But, once again, the tide turned when one boy yelled out, "What's it look like?" followed by "Tell us about it. Tell us!" I had them!

I soon started searching the library for things to read. Strangely, I knew enough to pick picture books, which, as most of you know, are sold and purchased for the little kids. The librarian wasn't too enthusiastic about my choices but that didn't stop me. I was delirious with joy over my newly found world of children's literature. I felt a sense of total freedom and started choosing everything from picture books, including alphabet and counting books, to poetry and novels. I tried not to leave anything out as I started to build a library in my classroom. The kids were astounded by the creativity and uniqueness of the writers and illustrators. Who would have thought that studying illustrators would generate so much enthusiasm?

I'll never forget the eagerness and fun of discovery that we all shared in that little classroom. The Judith Viorst books were pure magic, along with *Me and Caleb* and *Me and Caleb Again* by Franklin E. Meyers. I remember when I read these two books how I told the kids that in each book there was a very sad chapter, and I would let them know when I was going to read it in case anyone wanted to leave the room. In all the years no one ever left. Sure, there were a few tears, but they were tears of understanding, identification, and, most importantly, they were tears that we shared.

Then there was *Tales of a Fourth Grade Nothing* and *Freckle Juice* by Judy Blume, and *How to Eat Fried Worms* by Thomas Rockwell, *Freaky Friday* and *A Billion For Boris* by Mary Rogers, *the Button Boat* by Glendon Swarthout and, of course, *Sounder* by William Armstrong. We discovered *Julie of the Wolves* by Jean Craighead George, *Dorp Dead* by Julia Cunningham, which kept everybody on the edges of their chairs, *Where the Red Fern Grows* by Wilson Rawls, *The Planet of Junior Brown* by Virginia Hamilton, *Hey Dummy,* which took their breaths away, by Kin Platt. We laughed and loved every moment of *Soup* and *Soup and Me* by Robert Newton Peck. I know they'll never forget *Hang Tough Paul Mather* by Alfred Slote, and *A Day No Pigs Would Die* another by Robert Newton Peck. We'll never forget *A Taste of Blackberries* by Doris Smith and, oh, my, did we ever love *The Best Christmas Pageant Ever* by Barbara Robinson. I think the first line of this book was written for teachers, not kids—"The Herdmans were absolutely the worst kids in the history of the world." If you don't understand that line then I don't think you've been there long enough.

All teachers must face a family of "Herdmans" before their careers end. It's inevitable. Please, can someone tell me how come your own Mr. and Mrs. Herdman never have just one kid? They just keep coming and coming—one for every year, or so it seems.

In our school, Mr. and Mrs. Herdman had six kids in six years. They never took a year off. Don't they know the teachers need a breather even if they don't? Every September before the kids came, the whole faculty would go to the principal on bended knee with home-made cakes, pies, and jams and beg him not to give us a Herdman. You knew that if you got a Herdman you were going to hang on by your fingertips every minute of the year.

After having three Herdmans in a row, I went to the principal on bended knee with cash in my hand. I said, "Please, I've had three already. Give the next three to Stella." He said, "Bill, you're going to have all six. They'll keep you humble." For six long years I knew every facet of humility.

There had to be one special book to end the year – a book to leave the kids spellbound and wanting more, so that they would continue to read during the summer months. I did it with Carol Beach York's *Takers and Returners*. Timing is everything. I waited for the last ten minutes of that last day to read. All eyes were glued to the book in my hand as I read that final line, "We were all losers." I closed the book and said, "Have a wonderful summer, kids. Come back and see me sometime." They just sat there quietly. I knew reading was alive and well, and that I had given them a gift. That year, and every year after, I got the warmest good-byes.

No Principalship

I never wanted to become a principal. I really knew from the very beginning that my place and my happiness would be in the classroom with the kids. Yet, like so many other male teachers, I got caught up in the old trap of connecting advancement with success. If I didn't move up the ladder to a principalship, I felt I would not be successful in my career. I never stopped to realize that there were many ways to advance in a classroom. The thinking on that particular subject is changing, and many more men, in particular, and women are staying in the classroom by choice, but we still have a way to go. I hope that someday we can get rid of that kind of thinking and realize that we can have wonderful careers in the classroom, that we can be totally successful without moving into administration. Of course, in all fairness, many people seek the administrative level because of the monetary rewards, and they do a fine job. They just might be a little more content in a classroom if only a little more money and recognition were given.

It's good to see some of the intelligent women with administrative skills being accepted at the administrative level. For too long discrimination kept some exceptional people from demonstrating their ability to take a leadership role. We have some outstanding female educational leaders who have earned their positions on their own merit and are bringing new insights into the role of administration. The token females, in most cases, don't survive for obvious reasons.

I was on the treadmill to becoming a principal before I ever knew what hit me. I was making all the right moves like taking the right courses, becoming elected vice-president of the teacher's association, and even becoming the assistant principal (without pay, of course) in our building. My road was paved, and I was on my way, although not too comfortable about the whole trip.

Then, everything changed. It all happened very quickly on a Friday afternoon. Friday is not a good day for changes of any kind. Our principal was gone for the day, and I was in charge. About mid-afternoon the school secretary knocked at my door and said we had a slight problem. One of the neighbors just called and said that during recess time one of our students had gone to the bathroom on her lawn. I just told the secretary to tell the woman that we understood the problem, and that as soon as the principal returned on Monday everything would be taken care of. I then went back to try to make it through the last hour.

About fifteen minutes later there was an hysterical woman at my door. Her hair was in curlers; she was crying and yelling, and I do believe she was ready to hit me. She screamed, "Sir! Did you get my message?" I told her that I had indeed gotten her message, and I reminded her that my response was that the principal would handle everything when he got back. She said, "Sir! I don't think you know what happened." Trying to remain calm and cool I replied, "I certainly do." "Tell me what happened," she said. I said, "One of our students urinated on your lawn." She started screaming so loudly that I'm sure the whole school heard her. "Oh, no!" she began, "One of your students shit on my lawn and then threw it at me! Now, just what are you going to do about it?" After recovering from the shock of her revelation, I did my best to calm her down and assure her that I'd take care of the problem immediately. That seemed to satisfy her, although she was still steaming.

I then started my detective work, reluctantly. I went

from classroom to classroom to find out who had been at recess. The minute I opened the door to a particular classroom, one little guy yelled out, "I didn't throw it at her, Mr. Halloran." Case closed. The minute I walked back into my classroom a few of my livelier students yelled out, "Who threw the shit, Mr. Halloran?"

Friday afternoons like that one I didn't need. When I got home and Phyllis asked, "So how was your Friday?", I'm sure you know just what I replied. "SHITTY!" I couldn't help it. It was. That's when I told her that I definitely was not going to go for a principalship. She just quietly said, "I could have told you that a long time ago." "Grrrrrrrrr!"

As I look back, I now realize that a little boy and a screaming lady were responsible for my final decision. I was meant to do other things that would eventually bring me to work very closely with many fine principals. It takes a very special person to be an effective administrator, just as it takes a very special person to be a teacher, consultant, or what have you. The important thing is for each of us to earnestly try to find just the right job for just the right reasons before we find ourselves locked in a job we hate.

Robert

As I mentioned before, my first year of teaching was filled with excitement and challenges. Little did I know that there would be a few surprises, too. One of the biggest surprises and challenges came when the guidance department called me and asked if I would tutor a young junior high boy who was not allowed to leave his home. He wasn't even allowed to go outside his home for any reason, including school. If I would tutor him for one hour each day after school, I would be paid seven dollars an hour.

I remember feeling so honored to have been asked to do the job. Just think, my first year and my reputation had already spread throughout the city. And I would get seven dollars an hour. I'd be rich in no time.

What the guidance department failed to tell me was that I was the sixth teacher they had asked. All the others had refused, so they decided to ask me, the unsuspecting, enthusiastic, new teacher who accepted and rushed right in. They also forgot to tell me that the boy was a problem student, and that no one had been able to handle him so far. I should have known something was wrong by the mere fact that he couldn't leave his home, but what did I know at that time? Apparently not much.

I don't know what I was ever thinking of that first day. I went to the house with my grammar book and math book. I was going to teach thirty minutes of grammar and thirty minutes of math. Wrong! The minute I entered the house I knew I was in trouble. The house was in shambles. It smelled. There were dozens of cats everywhere.

The "wicked witch of the west" answered the door and

ushered me into the dining room, where a young boy with a sad pimply face sat with his head lowered. In a rough cold voice she said, "Here he is. He's all yours."

I sat down across from the boy and did my best to warm things up by chit-chatting with him for a few minutes. It didn't work. I was doing all the chitting and the chatting. The boy continued to sit and stare at the table. Being the new talented teacher on the block, I began teaching fractions. After thirty minutes of doing fractions by myself—even getting one wrong— I quickly swung into thirty minutes of nouns by myself. He just sat there, never looking up, never uttering a sound. But I went right on! To add to my dilemma, the "wicked witch," the boy's grandmother, was sitting in the living room yelling out about how terrible and dumb this kid was. Add to that, cats crawling everywhere. I sat back and thought, "No wonder nobody wanted to come here. What am I doing here?"

What the hell was I going to do? I could quit, but then I didn't want to tell the guidance department that I couldn't do the job. After all, my reputation was at stake. So I stayed. The rest of the week was as disastrous as the first day. I continued to do math and grammar by myself. I was improving in math. Robert just sat there as the cats continued to crawl and the witch continued to yell. After the first week I was slightly out of my mind. Talk about blood money!

Late Sunday night a feeling of gloom fell over me. I dreaded having to go to that house with those cats and that disagreeable woman. I was determined not to give up and, inside of me, I kept comparing my misery to that of Robert's. I concluded that, as bad as it was, I was far better off than he. Still, I was depressed.

After a rather silent dinner, Phyllis said, "Why don't you put away the math and grammar books and do something fun with the poor kid. He probably hates the stuff as much as you hate trying to teach it." She followed with, "What are you doing with your sixth graders that they love best of all?" I responded with, "I'm reading *Charlie and the Chocolate Factory* to them." Phyllis suggested that I read *Charlie* to Robert. She reminded me that I didn't have much to lose and so very much to gain. To convince me she told me it would either be *Charlie* or another week of solitary math and grammar.

The next day I went to Robert's house with only one book, *Charlie and the Chocolate Factory*, and a new attitude. Upon entering the house, I told "the witch" that if she continued to interrupt the lessons I would refuse to go there anymore, and that the guidance department would not pay for a replacement. I reminded her that by state law she would have to pay for a private tutor out of her own pocket. I didn't even know if that were true, but it certainly took care of "the witch." One problem was taken care of with one to go.

As I entered the dining room Robert sat, as usual, with his head down looking so very sad and lost. I remember thinking, "How did he ever get this way?" None of that mattered now. He was this way, and I had to do something about it if I possibly could. I didn't even attempt to speak to him. I just sat down and began to read *Charlie*. At the end of the hour I got up, said good-bye, and left.

I did the same thing for the next three days. If nothing else, it was better for me than math and grammar. I suspect it was better for Robert, too. By Friday I was feeling a little annoyed, even angry with Robert. I had conquered "the witch", but I couldn't conquer him. I went in, sat down, and placed *Charlie* on the table in front of me. I obviously thought that I could be just as stubborn as he was. How quickly one can revert to childish actions.

After a few minutes, Robert's head came up for the very first time. He looked at me and said, "Aren't you going to read *Charlie* today?" "I didn't know if you liked it," I replied. He paused a moment and then said, "I do." I could hardly believe it. Not wanting to lose the power of the moment, I said, "Okay, I'll read but only if you look up at me while I'm reading. You have wonderful eyes, and I have to see them in order to make the story exciting." I saw just the slightest smile, and he never took his beautiful eyes off of me for the entire hour.

I spent one of the best parts of my career with Robert. We did our math and grammar, and we read many books together. I discovered he was bright, friendly, and he had a terrific sense of humor. He was very special to me. I was special to him.

The following year Robert was put in a home for problem boys. I never saw him again, but for the next five years at Christmas time I received a card with just one word written at the bottom: ROBERT.

Twenty years have passed, and Robert must now be in his thirties. Sometimes I think about him and all the other "Roberts" of the world, and I am sad for what often is and what could be. I'm happy, too, when I think of the special moments we shared. I hope that by some miracle this book falls into his hands. He'll know he's the Robert I've written about. I learned a lot about Robert that year, and I learned a lot about myself. I sometimes wonder which of us was the better teacher.

Meeting the Authors

I want to tell you about a few of the authors I have met along the way. After twenty years of being involved with children's literature I've met quite a few. But you have to remember that in the early days of my teaching career I had never met an author. To me it was like a child meeting a famous movie star. I must admit that I'm still pretty much in awe of the creative talents of the people who give us such outstanding and unique books. It amazes me how these storytellers can capture kids and adults at the same time. It really tells us something, doesn't it?

The first author I was to meet turned out to be Robert Newton Peck. I had just finished reading *Soup* by Peck to my fifth graders, and they absolutely loved the book. At the end they begged for more. Having finished the book on the Friday before spring break, I thought it would be a great time to review letter writing by writing to Peck. On the back flap of the book it said that he lived in Darien, CT. I told the kids to really let him know what they thought about his book, about Soup and Rob, and all their wonderful adventures. I told them we would put the letters in the mail that very day. I suggested that with a little luck there might be a reply from Peck waiting for us when we got back to school a week later.

Excitement was running high. The kids wrote wonderful letters, candidly telling of their feelings. Then we all walked to the mailbox together. Before we parted, I told the kids to cross their fingers for the whole week, and maybe we'd have a letter from "Rob" next week. They all went home with crossed fingers. Suddenly I thought, "What have I done? Parents will be in the emergency room trying to get their kids' fingers uncrossed!" It might sound silly but you do know that kids are like that, don't you? I was just as excited as the kids. I just knew there'd be a letter waiting for us.

I'll never forget that Tuesday evening of spring break. I was sitting in the living room when the phone rang. In a kiddingly sarcastic voice I said, "Phyllis, if that's Robert Newton Peck calling, tell him I'm too busy to talk." Phyllis answered the phone, and then, without the slightest change of expression, handed the phone to me saying, "It's for you." Taking the phone, I said, "Hello." An unfamiliar voice said, "Hello! This is Robert Newton Peck calling." I think my heart stopped for a moment. He continued by saying, "I just received the letters from your kids. They're wonderful! They're the first letters I've ever received from kids." I just remained silent. Then he put the frosting on the cake. He said, "Will you come to New York and have lunch with me on Friday?"

Just think of what I could tell my kids on Monday morning. It would be a magical day. I would ask Peck all about Soup, Rob, Miss Kelly, and especially about Janice Riker. My kids would want me to ask about all these wonderful characters. They'd expect me to come back with as much information as possible. I would have gold in my hands. It would be my first introduction to what I would later refer to as GLUE.

On Thursday I took the bus from Springfield, Massachusetts to Port Authority, New York. I wore old clothes going in so as not to waste my best. I wore jeans, polo shirt, and a windbreaker. But in my suitcase I had a beautiful new plaid suit and a yellow tie. I know it sounds awful but trust me—it was all in good taste for the time. Everything was going to be just right. This was a first and, I thought then, a once in a lifetime experience.

I was up early Friday morning anxiously waiting for

my noon meeting with Robert Newton Peck, THE AU-
THOR! I still couldn't believe it was happening to me.
Then, without warning, came the first shock. No shirt!
In my excitement and rush, I forgot to pack a shirt.
That left me with a plaid suit, striped polo shirt and
a yellow tie. Well, maybe no one would notice!!

Shock number two was not far behind. It was raining—
no, pouring – and I didn't have a raincoat or umbrella.
And when it rains in New York, cabs are impossible
to get. My big day was already starting to go down
the drain with the rain.

I was supposed to meet Peck at his office in the American Home Products building, which was many blocks
away from my hotel. It was getting late, and there was
no sign of the rain letting up. Of course, there were
no cabs in sight, so there was only one thing left to
do. I ran!

When I arrived at the American Home Products Building I was a sight to behold. Plaid suit, striped polo
shirt, yellow tie, and soaking wet. I squished my way
across a plush rug to the receptionist and said, "I'm
here to meet with Robert Newton Peck." She took a
long slow look at me from head to toe. Finally she said,
"Sit down. I'll call and see if he's in." I thought, "What
do you mean if he's in?" She returned with, "He'll be
right down."

It was lunch time, and dozens of people were pouring
out of the elevators to go to lunch. Not knowing what
Peck looked like, I thought I'd just sit and see if I could
pick him out. Suddenly, the elevator door opened and
out stepped a tall man in a light tan suit, cowboy hat,
boots, and string tie. "Not exactly your Madison Avenue executive, I thought. That has to be Peck." Then
I wondered if he would be able to pick me out. He
quickly scanned the lobby. Then, without hesitating,
he walked right over to me and said, "You must be Bill

Halloran." I really didn't know if I should be flattered or insulted. He said, "It's raining out." I said, "I know." He said, "We'll have to run." I said, "I know." Without warning he ran out the door and up Madison Avenue. So I ran out the door and up Madison Avenue after him. He has long legs. I have short legs. Do you get the picture? I was always half a block behind him. I just kept my eye on that fine cowboy hat.

We finally arrived at the restaurant. I was completely winded and drenched. I think it was the first time he took a really good look at me. He said, "Oh! I don't know if I'll be able to get you into this restaurant. It's rather formal." At that point I didn't care anymore. I think he must have realized it and slipped the head waiter a few dollars, because we finally got a table over in the corner out of the way. Obviously, the waiter tucked us out of the way so Peck's ten-gallon hat wouldn't embarrass the other diners.

We sat down and ordered. Then a very interesting thing happened. Peck looked up at me and said, "This is a very special day in my life." I thought he was going to say because he was meeting me—the wonderful teacher from Massachusetts. He continued, "Today is my sixteenth wedding anniversary." I couldn't believe it!! I then looked at him and said, "Robert Newton Peck, this is a very special day in my life. It's my sixteenth wedding anniversary." It was quite a coincidence, and to this very day I receive an anniversary card from Peck every year!

Many years have passed since that lunch in New York City, yet every time I think of it I smile because of the eager young teacher meeting a famous author for the first time.

The next author meeting was a surprise and an accident. I went down to our library to find something short that would be fun to read to the kids. I found that wonderful story that goes, "There was an old woman who swallowed a fly and was sure to die." This particular version was illustrated by Steven Kellogg. I had never seen any of Kellogg's work before. The illustrations were wonderful. They were so zany and full of warmth and humor, that I became a fan immediately.

When I brought the book back to the kids they loved the story and the illustrations as much as I did. We were all Steven Kellogg fans and went hunting for more of his books. We had a great time getting to know this special man who knew how to put so much into one picture.

Once again, on the back flap of the book jacket it said that Steven Kellogg lived in Sandy Hook, Connecticut. So, once again, we wrote our letters to a real live author and then waited and hoped for a reply. We didn't have to wait long. Four days later the most enthusiastic letter came from Steven Kellogg. We would be fans of his forever. We would eagerly await each new Kellogg book. That little personal touch (GLUE) means so much in teaching. It's what offers some of the real teaching moments. It's what the kids will remember the rest of their lives.

A few months passed and I was asked to go to Newtown, Connecticut to work with a group of thirty teachers on a Saturday morning. Well, you know what that's like. Saturday is so precious to teachers. I knew what they were feeling. After all, I was a teacher, too. I knew those thirty teachers would dread having to be there.

I arrived at the Newtown High School early that Saturday morning to set up my books and get ready to face thirty disgruntled teachers. Right away I ran into trouble with the custodians. They wouldn't let me in. They needed permission from the superintendent or the principal. I went right to the top. I called the superintendent and got him out of bed and, believe me, the top wasn't happy!

By the time I got back to the school, the custodians weren't too happy either. They had heard from the superintendent, and I'm guessing that it wasn't a pleasant call, because they were not very pleasant to me. Finally, they let me in, but they weren't about to help me move tables and chairs around in the library. So, I spent the next hour being a furniture mover. As Phyllis said, "They gave you a gift. Now you had something to grouse about." She was right. It took my mind off of the thirty unhappy teachers I was about to meet.

I knew I had better calm down and get myself together before the teachers started to arrive, so I locked the library door. No one was going to get in before 9:00 A.M. You do know there are always a few teachers who arrive at least two hours before the workshop? Not this day! They might arrive early, but they weren't going to get in. Suddenly, a knock came at the door. No way! No one was going to get in. Then another knock and then another. I charged over to the door, opened it and in a curt voice said, "Yes?" The gentleman standing in front of me said, "My name is Steven Kellogg. Could I come in and hear you this morning?" "Yes!"

I can hardly put into words what a thrill it was for me that morning in Newtown, Connecticut to show and talk about the books of Steven Kellogg with Steven sitting right there in the audience. At the end of the morning he asked me if I would like to go to his home and have lunch. "Oh, yes!" I silently prayed that it wouldn't rain and that he didn't wear a cowboy hat.

I think Steve and I knew right away that we would have a long and lasting friendship. From the start it seemed like such a natural friendship, for we had so much in common. We shared a love of kids and books. We shared a lot of the same feelings about education, too. To this day, Steven Kellogg is and always will be very much a part of my work. He is a valued friend.

I had such good luck writing letters to Robert Newton Peck and Steven Kellogg, that I decided to sit down and write a letter, without the kids, to Ezra Jack Keats. I loved his books so very much. I owned all of his books, but I wanted some GLUE. I wanted that personal touch. I wrote the letter thinking it would be a wonderful surprise for the kids if some day I walked in with a reply from Ezra Jack Keats. I mailed the letter and waited. This time I wasn't so lucky. Weeks passed. I was about to give up when I received a letter from an editor of *Teacher Magazine.* She told me she was a friend of Keats, and she had seen my letter. She went on to say that she was thinking of printing the letter in the magazine. But it was the P.S. that I really liked. Keats sent the message that if ever I were in New York City he would like to meet me and take me to lunch. Here we go again!

Well, Keats didn't know what I was like, because I went right to the phone and called him. The conversation went something like this:

"Hello, Ezra! This is Bill."

"Bill who?"

"Bill! The teacher you said you'd like to take to lunch if ever I were in New York. I'll be in New York next week. Where shall I meet you?"

I knew I had him trapped. He knew it, too. He finally said to meet him at the Illustrator's Club at noon and we'd have lunch. I quickly told him I'd be there. I didn't give a hoot about the lunch, but I wasn't going to let the chance to meet Ezra Jack Keats slip through my fingers.

Once again, I took the bus to New York City. This time I made sure I had a shirt and at least a dozen Keats books with me. I was into autographs, and I wanted him to write something wonderful and different in every book.

I must have been at the Illustrator's Club by 11:00 A.M. with suit, shirt, tie, books, and a pounding heart. I was like a ten year old kid about to meet his idol. I was going to meet one of the most famous authors and illustrators of children's books in the whole world. The clock started ticking away. It was soon 12:30, 12:45, 1:00, 1:15. All of a sudden I felt angry. "Sure," I thought, "if I were the editor from Harper & Row he would have been here by 11:00 A.M. He thinks I'm just an unimportant fifth grade teacher and doesn't care. I'll give him just two more hours!! If he doesn't show I'll never speak to him again!!"

At 1:30 the door opened and in walked Keats. I'm sure he could feel the anger. It really wasn't a joyful meeting, and we still had a lunch to get through. He tried to make conversation, but I wasn't giving in. I know how to pout, and I wasn't about to let him off the hook. The silence became very uncomfortable, and, I'm sure, out of desperation he began to talk about kids and the books he writes for them. I began to melt as one word fell upon the other. I liked what he was saying, and I wanted to hear more. By the time we got to dessert we were budding friends. I knew I was with a very special man. He then asked if I would like to go to his apartment and see his studio where he does his writing and illustrating. My answer required no extra thought.

It's almost impossible to put the rest of the afternoon into words. He showed me treasure after treasure and told me story after story. I think I'll just say it was one more very magical afternoon in my ongoing education and trust that you will understand. Oh, yes. He did sign all my books and wrote something different in each one.

Thinking back, I made two major mistakes with Ezra Jack Keats. It's still painful to talk about them. I don't think I'll ever forgive myself for being so insensitive to the moment. Keats asked me if I'd like to spend the next day with him at the Metropolitan Museum of Art. My reply was, "Thank you, but I have to go book buying." Why didn't I know that this was a once in a lifetime chance, and that I could go book buying any day of the week? I guess I had to make every minute and every penny count. As it was, I had to scrape together the bus and hotel money, and it was a chance to get into the best book stores.

The other mistake, which I can still hardly believe, occurred several weeks after our meeting. He wrote me a letter asking if I would be interested in collaborating on a book with him. Again, I was too busy with my career. I guess it was at a time in my life when I wasn't open for something like that. I just wasn't ready. I learned, the hard way, to grab for the gold ring as it comes around, because it so often doesn't come around again. Fortunately, there are all kinds of gold rings of all sizes and shapes, and I have my share.

I only saw Ezra once again before he died. It was at the American Library Association Conference in New York City. There were fifteen thousand librarians at the conference. I saw Keats surrounded by hundreds trying to get his autograph. It had been almost ten years since our meeting, and I wondered if he'd recognize or even remember me at all. I stood in line for over an hour. When it was my turn he looked up and said, "It's you!" I said, "Do you remember?" He told me he did not remember my name, but that he remembered the wonderful afternoon we had spent together talking about kids and books. He added that he hoped we might do that again sometime soon. I told him about how the meeting and spending time with him affected my teaching so much.

Just one month before Ezra died, mutual friends had planned a day for Phyllis and me to spend with Ezra and the woman he was seeing at the time. We were going to meet at the Connecticut shore and renew our friendship. Just before the meeting we got word of his death. Ezra Jack Keats was a very special and talented man, a giving man. I'm so thankful for that one afternoon.

It was a bleak February day, and I was sitting alone in a Holiday Inn somewhere in the country, depressed and feeling sorry for myself. By then I had been doing quite a bit of traveling, speaking about children's literature and reading. I had made up my mind that I wasn't going to accept one more speaking engagement. I had had it, and I needed some time off. I was so weary of hotels, restaurants, and airports. That was it! I would answer no more calls.

By the time I got home I was through indulging myself, but, in spite of feeling much better, I was still not about to accept any more speaking engagements. The phone rang. "No!," I thought, "I will be firm." No matter what the offer I would stand firm. The caller asked me to go to Cedar Rapids, Iowa to speak at a conference with Eric Carle. I gave my answer immediately and firmly. "yes!"

I just knew I had to meet and work with Eric Carle. He was, and still is, one of the most outstanding authors and illustrators in the world and had been a favorite of mine for such a long time. I owned and loved all of his books. Of course I would go. I had to go. It was another chance of a lifetime, and I knew it.

The big day came, and I flew to Cedar Rapids wondering what Eric Carle would be like. I was convinced, based upon his books, that he would be warm and sensitive, and that he would have a gentle sense of humor. We were to meet at dinner the night before the conference. I know it sounds strange, but we took to each other immediately. I think our friendship started right then and there with the first handshake. I knew we would be friends; I think he did, too. I must ask him sometime.

I was surprised and pleased to learn that Eric lived in Massachusetts, too, not far from Westfield. We flew home from the conference together having a great time swapping stories, discussing literature and world affairs, and sometimes just sitting quietly. That trip seemed to cement what I felt at our first meeting would be a solid relationship. Over ten years have passed since that meeting, and Eric has made my life rich with his friendship.

I remember sitting with Eric early one morning at another Holiday Inn in Houma, Louisiana having breakfast. The weather was unbearably hot. We were about to leave to teach all day. We hoped there would be air conditioning where we were going, but we almost knew that, even if there were, the system would be out of order. It was that kind of a morning. We were wilted before the day had really begun. All of a sudden Eric looked at me and in his quiet manner said, "Bill! Who finds these places for you? I feel like I'm at the edge of the world ready to fall off." We just sat there laughing for some time. Think about it. There we were, two men from Massachusetts wearing our ivy league clothes sitting on the edge of the world. It was a miracle that we didn't fall off.

Another highlight in the Eric Carle story is when his wonderful wife Bobbie gave him a birthday party. She gave him one of the most beautiful presents I've ever seen. About mid afternoon she called all their guests out onto the lawn dressed in brightly colored leotards waving beautiful colored silk scarves. The children, who were from the local schools, danced several of out onto the lawn dressed in brightly colored leotards waving beautiful colored silk scarves. The children, who were from the local schools, danced several of Eric's books. It was a perfect way to say, "Happy Birthday, Eric Carle!"

All through the years I have never given a speech without reading *Leo the Late Bloomer* by Robert Kraus. I think it is a very special book with a powerful message. Teachers and parents should read *Leo* often, especially the line, "Then one day, in his own good time, Leo bloomed!" We really need to study that line until we fully understand it and put its message into practice. How can we continue to force children to do things that nature hasn't intended that they do—yet. Blooming takes place at different times for every individual. Robert Kraus understood this, and, yet, so many of us do not.

It was an August afternoon, and it was hot. Phyllis and I were traveling in Connecticut with a day off in between destinations. As we drove through one of the lovely little towns, I recognized it as the place where Robert Kraus lived. I kiddingly said, "Phyllis, let's look up Robert Kraus in the phone book and then stop by for his autograph." We laughed and then looked at each other with the same thought in mind. "Lets."

We drove up to the front of his house, and I said, "Let's go ring the bell." Phyllis said, "You go." I said, "Come on. You'll miss all the fun of it." Again, she told me to go, so I went. I rang the bell and a lovely woman, who turned out to be Mrs. Kraus, came to the door. I told her who I was, and that I wanted to see Robert

Kraus. She told me he wasn't home but asked if she could help. I could hardly believe that I was standing there, never mind tell her how she could help. Finally I said, "I'm really a fan of your husband's, and I wanted to tell him that I love his books, especially *Leo the Late Bloomer.*" This must have caught her attention, because she said, "Would you like to come in?" "Oh, yes," I quickly answered, looking over my shoulder at Phyllis who was sitting in the hot car. After about thirty or forty minutes we asked Phyllis to come in!

It was wonderful sitting in the Kraus' beautiful living room, hoping Robert would walk through the door. Then Pamela Kraus asked us if we'd like some coffee or tea. We thanked her but said no. We didn't want her to go to any bother. It was too hot for coffee or tea anyway. Then she smiled and asked if we'd like something a little cooler! Let me tell you, we had the best afternoon with Pamela Kraus, and Robert never did come home. Pamela ended up autographing all of our books and even gave us a book for which she had done the illustrations. We heard the most wonderful stories from the gracious and spirited lady whom we will never forget.

When we were leaving, I asked Pamela if Robert were home would he have invited us in. She smiled and said, "Probably not." Later we did get to meet Robert, and he insisted that he would have let us. I think that's only because Pamela had set down the groundwork. Of course, we didn't miss the chance to tell him that our afternoon with his wife couldn't have been improved upon. In his own wonderful way he said, "You're probably right. The right Kraus went to the door that day." We don't get to see the Krauses very much, but we have warm memories of Pamela and a bond with Robert through *Leo the Late Bloomer.* And Robert did sign all the books—right under Pamela's name.

Part Three
Traveling Teacher

An Invitation

For as many years as I have been traveling, people have been asking me how I got started as a traveling educator. They often comment that they think it must be a very glamorous job, especially in the educational world. I would not call it glamorous, but it does have certain advantages, such as getting to meet thousands of teachers from all parts of the country and learning that we share a wonderful profession in spite of the problems that face us. I get to meet many authors and illustrators and even become friends with some of them. Meeting other traveling educators is still another advantage to this job, but, all things considered, it is like most jobs. I have my curriculum, my students, and my classroom. I must be prepared to be the best I can be. Just as in a traditional teaching environment, I encourage my students, the teachers of thousands of children, to want to learn by making learning interesting, relevant, and fun. Most of all, I hope my students will learn to honor themselves by being thinkers, by promoting the thinking process in their students before any set curriculum, and to work toward change when it is needed.

I would honestly have to say that some mornings I get up and ask myself, "How DID I get this job?" As I think back, it was rather strange the way it all happened.

A high school teacher in the system where I was working called me and asked if I'd speak to a group of teachers about reading. I refused immediately. I could never do that, or so I thought. Then he said, "Would you bring a box of books and tell the group how you get kids to read such books?" Well, that was more appealing, but I told him no more than ten teachers could come. Don't ask me why I limited the group to ten, because I don't know!

Maybe I felt that the situation was being taken out of my hands, and it was a way to have a bit of control. I'm just not sure.

So, one afternoon I spent a couple of hours with ten very interesting and interested teachers, talking about books and how to get kids to read. I can still remember how amazed and happy I was, as well as surprised, that the teachers liked my presentation. It was a good experience for me, and it encouraged me to keep doing what I was doing in my classroom.

A few weeks later I got another call asking me to give the same talk again. He asked if fifteen teachers could attend this time. It sounds so foolish, now, after having stood before hundreds, even thousands of people at one time. I did relent and allow fifteen to come, and this session went along as smoothly and enjoyably as the first.

After that second presentation, my phone kept ringing and ringing, and I kept going – evenings, saturdays, after school, and even during vacations. My colleagues kept asking me why I was doing all that extra work. I couldn't give any particular answer other than that it didn't seem like extra work, and that I enjoyed doing it. All I really knew for sure was that I had to keep talking about kids, reading, books, and how easy and important it was to bring all three together. It seems that we often make educational situations so difficult when they could be so simple and enjoyable.

Marathon Week

The weeks and months rolled by. The phone kept ringing, and I kept going. Then came the turning point. I walked into our teachers' room and on the bulletin board was a poster advertising Marathon Week at the University of Massachusetts. Anyone could call the University and offer to present a workshop, lecture, etc. as long as you were willing to do it without pay. All you had to do was give your topic and a description of your presentation so a time and place could be assigned to you. They did not guarantee that anyone would attend, but they were willing to give you a chance.

I'll never forget the night of the presentation. It was a cold, rainy night as Phyllis and I, along with Ina and Judy, two friends, dragged, pushed, and pulled boxes of books to the university. There must have been a thousand books in those boxes. To this day I travel with far too many books, but I know many of the teachers love to browse through the books after my presentation. My dream is to someday walk in with a briefcase like any other normal speaker. Somehow I really don't think that will ever happen. The books are so wonderful and special; I guess I have to have them with me. I've concluded from observation that the top-level consultants usually bring nothing more than a few transparencies for the overhead projector. What joy! I guess I'm not destined for that top level, because I'm not willing to give up my books. And now that I have stopped to think about it, there is great joy in knowing I'm bringing my books to thousands of teachers and, in turn, thousands of kids. It simply doesn't work to describe a book. To motivate kids we must be motivated first. Once most teachers see and feel the books, they are more apt to use them to motivate kids to read. I'm convinced that we will always need someone to bring the books to the teachers and the kids. What a heavy legacy to leave some poor unsuspecting person.

Back to the university and Marathon Week. I was assigned to the cafeteria.I set out all the books and waited nervously. "What if no one shows up?", I thought. "What if more than ten people show up?" These and other foolish questions raced through my mind, as I carefully went over my table of books again and again.

Finally, about one hundred people came to hear about children's books that night. Imagine my surprise, my joy, and my fear! I didn't really know how to start so, without looking, I reached behind me and grabbed a book. It was *Make Way for Ducklings* by Robert McCloskey. I remember talking about those wonderful ducks, about Robert McCloskey, and about McCloskey's important contribution to children and reading. I was off and running! I spoke nonstop for two hours that night. Those of you who have ever been with me know I can do that! Sometimes, especially when the audience is with me, I think I could go ten hours without taking a breath. In that respect, Phyllis compares me to Al Jolson.

I don't remember too much else about that night except that my audience clapped for a long time at the end of my presentation. I can still remember how thrilling it was to have talked to one hundred strangers about the books I loved and to have done it successfully.

Marathon Week was just the beginning. A week later I received a letter from the Darien, Connecticut School System asking me to go to Darien and say the very same thing I had said that night at the university. Now here's the unexpected part; they offered to pay me! Unbelievable! But how could I ever accept money for something I loved to do? I would be embarrassed. Actually, it wasn't embarrassing at all.

A new door was opening for me. I went to Darien three or four times, and on one of those days I met Joanna Nicholson, Bena Kallick and June Gould from the Teacher Center at Fairfield University. At the end of my speech they came up to me and asked me to speak at the Teacher Center. At the time I didn't realize that I was meeting three people who were dedicated to giving kids the best education possible. It is almost twenty years later, and they are still hard at work, each in different ways, enriching the lives of kids.

By this time, Phyllis had started giving presentations, too. Together we went to Fairfield University many times, dragging the books through ice, snow, sleet, and sunshine. Fairfield University was slowly becoming home to us, because Joanna, Bena, and June believed in us and our work. We have been adjunct professors at Fairfield University for fifteen years.

Cardboard Boxes

After Darien, I continued to teach fifth grade and, in my free time, give talks on kids and books. This lasted for a few years until, again, another kind of door opened for me that resulted in my having to make a very big decision.

It was 7:00 o'clock on a Saturday morning when the phone rang. A man on the other end asked me to fly to Dallas, Texas and speak about books for ninety minutes. I thought the man was crazy or that it was a crank call. I learned very quickly that the man was not crazy, nor was he making a crank call. He turned out to be the president of Educational Consulting Associates, the leading consulting firm in the country at the time. Talk about being naive! I didn't even know there was a consulting circuit in education on such a grand scale. I truly did not appreciate the opportunity that was being offered to me that morning.

I told the man that I had never given a presentation out of driving distance before, and that I didn't know how to get all my books to Texas. I'll never forget what he said or his tone of voice. Slowly and deliberately he said, "My good man, get yourself some cardboard boxes, put your books in the boxes, tape the boxes, check the boxes on an airline, and fly to Texas." I said, "Oh." And I did just what he said. After Texas he asked me to speak in Denver and New York City. He then offered to sponsor me in one hundred cities in this country and Canada. I turned him down and went back to my fifth grade.

At that time, I had no desire to do anything but be a good classroom teacher and to share my love of books with local teachers who were interested. As I said earlier, I was unaware of the consulting world, for I had never been exposed to it before. Why would I ever give up what I had and loved for what I didn't know and had no feelings for?

Bill Martin, Jr.

Then another opportunity knocked at my door or rang my bell, I should say. One Sunday afternoon I got a call from a man named Bill Martin, Jr. asking me to go to Minot, North Dakota and work with him for one week. He told me that a mutual friend had told him about me, and that he was interested in having someone like me teach with him at a college where he gave an annual course.

I don't know if I can adequately explain my excitement at that time. Bill Martin, Jr. was someone I admired greatly. All of his materials for children were so unique. He was a very creative and talented man who was trying to stay within the realm of the accepted format for the language arts program, yet breathe some much needed life into it. He so obviously knew that kids should be exposed to the skills and appreciations that it took the rest of the educational world years to discover—and only after the mind/brain research started to reach the surface. Here was a man who understood and believed in what I was doing. This was the man whose suggestions and materials I had used with great success. He made teaching a lot easier and a lot more enjoyable. He was, and still is, an advocate of the love of words and stories. I believe Bill Martin, Jr. has always been a man ahead of his time. He was a pioneer of the holistic realm of education. The true test of his worth is that he has endured and, to this day, enjoys the respect, admiration, and cooperation of the classroom teacher, the one who has the greatest task of all. There is no greater honor.

I had always heard such great things about this man. Now he was on the phone asking me to travel and teach with him. In my amazement I said, "You don't know anything about me or what I really do." He replied, "You love books, don't you? You believe that kids and books belong together, don't you? That's all I need to know. I'll see you in North Dakota."

On the day I went to ask permission to go I was angry before I got there, because I was so sure I'd be denied. To my complete surprise I was understood and supported. Imagine my excitement when I heard the words, "You must go. This is a wonderful opportunity for you and for our school system." Later, when discussing the whole situation with Carl, my principal, I was surprised again when he said, "Bill, don't you realize that you won't be here at this school much longer?" To tell you the truth, I hadn't ever really thought about it. I guess the present was so good for me, that I never looked to the future in those days.

E.C.A. and Bill Martin, Jr. provided me with some of the most meaningful and exciting days of my career. Everyone always says that the beginning of the climb towards success is the most exciting. For me it was the most exciting—not necessarily the best—but the most exciting.

On my way to North Dakota I had to change planes in Chicago. While I was waiting to board the plane a man was pacing up and down in front of me making me very nervous. I remember thinking, "I wish he would light somewhere." I knew if I held on a few more minutes I'd be rid of him. You guessed it! He was assigned to the seat right in front of me. In the middle of my silent moan a funny thing happened. A woman walked down the aisle, stopped beside the man in front of me, and said, "Bill Martin, Jr., how are you?" Before I knew what I was doing I said, "You're Bill Martin?" The man turned, looked at me and said, "And I'll bet you're Bill Halloran." That was how we finally met. Of course we laughed and talked, and a bond started to grow between us that exists to this day.

The week at Minot State College was exciting and joyful. I met wonderful people, and I was part of an exciting educational experience. Bill had a way of getting everyone to do their best and to like the feeling it gave them.

One thing especially stands out in my mind about that week. Bill announced to all of us that at the end of each day we would have a "happy hour." How wonderful! I had never been in a course where the day ended with a happy hour. My joy was not to last, for Bill's idea of a happy hour and my idea of a happy hour were two different things. Bill's idea was to have the participants of the course get up on the stage at the end of each day and perform by sharing a song, a piece at the piano, a poem, etc. Thursday afternoon was the day set aside for the staff to get up on the same stage and perform. As you can probably guess, my idea of "happy hour" included a glass and some ice cubes.

Once I got over my disappointment, I had to seriously consider my participation in Thursday's activities. No way was I ever going to get up on a stage and perform in front of hundreds of people. I had never been on a stage to do something like that in my life. I was not about to start now. I spent most of my time trying to avoid the "clipboard girl." It was her job to go around and sign everyone up for their contribution to "happy hour." If your name went on the clipboard you were doomed. You had no other choice than to perform.

Early Thursday morning I thought I was home free. That is, until I got clipped, so to speak. The devious nature of the "clipboard girl" came to light when she stepped out in front of me from nowhere and simply said, "Okay, Bill, what'll I put down for you? You do want to participate, don't you?" I said, "I'd be thrilled." Now what the hell was I going to do?

Unknowingly, Phyllis came to my rescue once more. Before I left home she had given me a wonderful teddy bear story to add to my workshop presentation if I thought it would fit in. I had barely had a chance to read through it once, but I remember liking it. So I picked it up again hoping it would be appropriate to share with the group. After all, that's what I do. So, I opened up *Ira Sleeps Over* by Bernard Waber, read it, and decided that I would read it for my presentation at "happy hour."

Three o'clock arrived, and all the staff members sat in the front row of the auditorium waiting for the joy of "happy hour" to begin. The first two staff members got up on the stage and gave a memorable performance of readings from Shakespeare. I started to sweat. The next person played a piano concerto. I thought, "Oh, no! I'm going to be sick!" What the hell was I thinking of? I couldn't follow them with a teddy bear story. "I know!" I thought, "I'll throw up and leave. The audience will surely understand that an ill man can't perform."

Suddenly I heard that "clipboard girl" call my name, and I found myself walking up the stairs and then to center stage. I nervously peered at what looked like a million people. I thought, "How the hell did I ever get myself into this?" Of course, there was no way out, so I did what I always do when I'm in a tight spot; I took a deep breath and decided to let the chips fall where they may.

As I began with that wonderful first line, "I was invited to sleep at Reggie's house.", my voice sounded distorted, almost as if I were speaking in an empty cavern in slow motion. The rest was a blur. At the end I remember walking off the stage and back to my seat. All of a sudden a teddy bear story received a standing ovation. Thank God for teddy bears and Bernard

Waber.

Bill Martin, Jr. will always be a special man in my life. He took a risk on an unknown who simply loved children's books. He gave me a chance by believing in me and the power of books. In addition, he gave me the best advice ever for this type of job. He told me to always keep my feet on the ground and to always fight getting a swelled head. He said, "Be there for the people. Be a teacher. Always take time to listen and, most importantly, be willing to share your limelight. Surround yourself with people of talent, give them a break whenever possible, and let their success flow to the kids, too." It was good advice, Bill, and I've done my best.

The times were exciting but hectic. The excitement of Bill Martin, Jr., the calls and pressure from Educational Consulting Associates, and the phone that kept ringing for me to do local presentations kept me happily on the go. I loved it all no matter how tired or frustrated I got.

Discovering the
Power of Books

An interesting adventure, to say the least, began one day in Carl's office. I was told that there was a group that wanted me to give an evening presentation, and that I should return the call and definitely accept the offer. Carl added that he thought it would be a good experience for me. When I inquired as to the nature of the group and the request, he simply looked at me for a moment and said, "Just call." That made me suspicious.

I placed the call, and I was told that the group was made up of special people. Of course, I asked, "What kind of special people?" I found out that some in the group were emotionally disturbed, some were experiencing nervous breakdowns, some were alcoholics, and a few were drug addicts. My response was, "Are you sure you have the right Bill Halloran?" "You're the one who talks about kids' books, aren't you?" he asked. Very softly I told him I was, to which he replied that I was indeed the one he wanted. Because I was taken aback by the man's request, I told him that I would have to call him back. Almost immediately upon hanging up something told me to put aside my reservations and say yes. That's just what I did.

I'll never forget the night of that presentation as long as I live. As I drove to the inner city I couldn't help but wonder what was ahead for me. I walked into the building with great trepidation. I heard the sound of mixed voices and followed those voices until I came to a group of about forty people. Although many of the people looked at me when I entered the room, there was no one to greet me. I was never acknowledged, and there was no conversation between me and anyone. My first thought was to turn and walk away, but instead I went about the business of setting out some five hundred books, talking to each one as I put it down.

Finally, someone came over and told me to sit with the group while they had their weekly business meeting. With my heart pounding, I did as I was told. The meeting began, and almost immediately there was a fight over missing funds. There was yelling and name calling over some mixup in regard to who was to do what for several different upcoming events. One woman sat in a trance sucking on her hair, while the group got louder and louder. The one in charge finally came over to me and said with absolutely no expression in his voice, "Why don't you begin?" I remember thinking right at that moment, "There's going to be one dead principal when I get to school tomorrow!" I also remember thinking how Bill Martin, Jr.'s "happy hour" was a piece of cake compared to this.

I stood up and said, in what I thought was a good loud voice, "If you will all come down to the other end of the room with me, we can begin." I then turned and walked to the end of the room. I can still feel the surprise and the panic that set in when I turned to begin, and not one person had followed me. As a matter of fact, everyone was still at the other end of the room yelling and fighting. I did the only thing that was going to keep me from running. I began to speak. I started with joke books, as I usually do. Let me tell you, it was strange reading jokes and riddles with no one there. I just kept going. I was in my own twilight zone. I read a few poems, and then I started to read *Alexander's Terrible, Horrible, No Good, Very Bad Day* by Judith Viorst. All of a sudden it started. One by one they began drifting down to my end of the room and sat very still and very close to me. I guess they could relate to that kind of a day.

I talked about books for over two hours that night, showing beautiful picture books, reading poems, and telling funny stories from my classroom. The wonderful people in that room became my classroom children for two magical hours and then some. It proved, once more, the power of books. There was no need for age, grade, and ability levels. It had to do with enjoyment, fulfillment, and the love of reading.

By the end of the evening, everyone tried to help me pack my books and walk me to my car. I was made club member number 87 and was invited to the dance that was to be held the following week. I was told that if I didn't have a date they'd take care of everything. What a night and what an experience. I learned so much about people, myself, and books in one short evening.

Taking a Risk

Well, E.C.A. called again saying this would be their final offer to sponsor me in one hundred cities in the United States and Canada. They gave me two days to think it over. I really didn't want to accept their offer. It took me so long to get my classroom, and I was happy there. I loved the kids, and I loved teaching. I did not want to give up my life in the classroom. I decided not to leave.

Once again, Phyllis entered the picture. She reminded me that I was almost forty, and that if I were ever going to take a chance it would have to be now. She told me that she felt that I was meant to share the love of reading, so that uninspired teachers, jaded teachers, and new teachers could go back and share that love with thousands and thousands of kids and feel good again about teaching. She said that many teachers needed to be reaffirmed, to be openly supported in what they inwardly knew to be the way to teach reading. She said that I should go and do the job I was obviously meant to do and reminded me that so few people ever realize their calling or ever have the opportunity to follow it. Phyllis, Beth and I talked it over, and we all agreed that it would be the right thing to do. So, the week before the opening of school I called my principal and said, "I quit! I'm going on the road." He said, "You're crazy!" I said, "Tell Phyllis."

I signed a contract with E.C.A. and began my one-hundred city tour with five heavy-duty cardboard boxes with one hundred books to a box. It would take a full year to complete the tour, and then I would have to look for another job. It was a one year deal. Sometimes I still can't believe I did it. I left a lot of security. I left tenure, a retirement plan, and Blue Cross. I thought, on various occasions, that I could easily be throwing it all out the window, especially my Blue Cross! The surprising thing was that once I took the final step and gave up my security, so to speak, I experienced a great freedom and was never afraid to take a chance again. Taking that risk was the first of many risks I was to take.

At the time, I really did not fully understand just what I was getting into. I didn't know that exhaustion, anxiety, stress, and depression would be my traveling companions from time to time, along with the euphoria. I never realized how difficult it could be to stand in front of your peers every day and try to motivate them. I was a fairly sheltered guy who wondered how anyone could not want to know about the beautiful books and the talented people who wrote and illustrated them. I was so surprised to find out that children are much easier to motivate than adults. I never knew what it would be like to look into hundreds of eyes every day. People talk to you with their eyes, and sometimes what they say is surprising and reveals a lot about the unhappy teachers that are with our children. To this day, I cannot understand how teachers, of all people, cannot enjoy the books or how they can disagree with reading to kids. Something is very wrong in a school system that produces teachers who do not have time to read, who are unwilling to read, or who are not allowed to read to their children. Fortunately, most teachers understand and believe the importance of literature, even if they don't fight for the right to include it in their curriculum daily. We have to learn to be more forceful about what we know, through experience, to be necessary.

There were days when I thought I was going to drop in my tracks going from city to city, but for some strange reason that I can't explain, I had a drive inside of me that wouldn't quit. To this day I have that drive, and I do more cities now than when I started. I guess when you know you're making a contribution and affecting the lives of kids, you have to go on. When I hear from teachers who thank me for giving them courage to do what they know is the right thing to do, I feel it's all worthwhile. I'm amazed at how many letters I get from teachers and parents who thank me for enriching their lives with the books. Of one thing I am certain—that thousands of kids get read to because of me and others like me. That alone makes the long flights, cold meals, and hard mattresses worthwhile.

At the same time it was exhilarating to call home and share with Phyllis all the enthusiastic audiences, outstanding teachers, authors, illustrators, and beautiful parts of the country that I got to experience. Sometimes we would talk for hours, or I would talk and she would listen as I described for her my wonderful experiences. It was all very exciting for us, and, although I worked for E.C.A. for one hundred days, I accepted invitations from many other people and systems to speak at conventions, in-service days, and even to people in the business world.

As I went about my business, every day was different. Each new city brought new and different experiences – mostly good. I was certainly seeing the country and a lot of airports and Holiday Inns. I could walk in, turn on the lights and take a shower with my eyes closed. Every room is laid out precisely the same way. I'd run into trouble when I thought I was in a Holiday Inn but was actually in some other motel.

I had to get used to the fact that everything would not go according to plan, my plan, as I traveled. That was not easy, because I am a very organized person, and I expect that everyone else is, too. Not so! I'd get to some motels or hotels and they wouldn't even know I was coming, which could mean my speaking room could possibly have poor light or no heat. The chairs could be in the wrong arrangement, or there could be too few chairs. The room could be too hot or too cold. It was often a hassle, and still is, but I've learned to accept it even though I wish it were otherwise. I think I must hold the record for speaking at the Holiday Inns. It's been thirteen years, and I'm still here—or there. I think they should make me an executive and give me a percent of the action.

In a way, I was falling into a trap without knowing it. When I spoke at the Holiday Inns people came to hear me, and then some would hire me to go to their school system for in-service. I soon realized that the Holiday Inn route was a showcase for me. If I stopped speaking at the hotels, my private work would eventually fall off, and I'd soon be unemployed. It wasn't vicious, but it was a cycle. I would love to get off the hotel circuit and just do private work, but for me I don't think that will ever happen. I really shouldn't complain, though. I'm out there reaching thousands of kids through the educators I meet, and that's just what I want to do. Many wonderful consultants didn't last because they didn't stay with the one day workshops. Things change very quickly in education, and your visibility is your ticket to ride. I grouse a lot, but I'm very content, and I count myself as fortunate to still be doing what I want to do.

At the end of the first year E.C.A. offered me another one hundred cities. I gave the offer careful consideration and then took it, because I carefully considered the fact that I had no other job. One other very important fact was considered—I liked what I was doing. So it was once more around the block. This second year ended with my working in Europe. Phyllis and Beth were invited as guests of E.C.A. It was another great experience for the three of us.

By then I had given up the cardboard boxes and had graduated to five aluminum cases. For me, that was progress. Those aluminum cases looked intriguing and prompted many questions from fellow travelers. Often at baggage claim I would be asked, as subtly as possible, just what I was carrying in the cases. At first I told them exactly what I had and then felt compelled to explain. That turned into a problem, because I would find myself being pulled into giving a mini-workshop. So I started improvising. One day I would be carrying "my rock collection." Another day it would be "my coin collection." On one particular occasion I made a mistake which, had I not corrected quickly, could easily have prevented me from writing this book. I told the cab driver that I was transporting gold. Need I say more? I never knew for some time that, as I was getting into a cab, a colleague of mine told an inquirer that I was a famous dancer, and my costumes were in my cases!

That second year was not an easy one for me, but as I look back on it, it was my own fault. I became fanatical about things being just right at the hotels and, of course, they never were. Eventually I learned to relax and go with the flow. I wasted a lot of good energy, because everything always did turn out fine in the end. However, in defense of my fanaticism, I was told many times by participants at my presentations or by people in charge of programs that I was so organized it was a pleasure for them. I know I'll always feel that I owe my audiences the best I can give them, and that means being prepared, being on time, having comfortable surroundings, and sticking to the time schedule. Unfortunately, I was not always able to provide the best possible conditions at the different speaking sites. To this day I am amazed at how many people are concerned with ice water, coffee, hot air, cold air, etc., never realizing that what is a warm room to one person is a cold room to another. It could make a person crazy. Such wasted energy!

By the time my second year was over, I had sharpened my speaking skills greatly. I knew how to be in front of an audience of five or five hundred. I knew about timing, pacing, humor, and using my whole body to teach, from facial expressions to a particular wave of the arm or a certain stance to make a point. It all came very naturally to me. The more I spoke, the more the necessary elements of expression appeared.

I do know that from time to time people would try to imitate me, and they did so unsuccessfully. That never works. You have to be natural, to develop your own style. Often when Phyllis and I are working together, people expect her to be as animated as I am. It would be disastrous for her, for it's not her style, and eventually people stop expecting me and appreciate her own unique way of presenting. As a matter of fact, some people take great delight in telling me that Phyllis is really good, maybe even a little better than I am. I have a pat answer for that—"Yes, she is. Now sit down and be quiet!"

Toward the end of the second year I flew to the E.C.A. office in Denver, Colorado to negotiate a new contract for a third year. The Company wanted me, because I had become a money maker for them. It was a label I always hated, but I knew it was part of the reason they were willing to sponsor me. It was business. In all fairness to E.C.A., they were an educational outfit that always tried to give the people the best educationally, in spite of their being a business. From the president on down, everyone tried to make a meaningful educational contribution to the country, and they did.

Although I made a good deal of money for the Company, I made little for myself and my family. Many people think that I made huge sums of money when I started out. On the contrary, I had to earn my way up the ladder in visibility as well as in money matters. People think that I just walked right in and commanded a top salary, as some try to do today and fail. Well, I did make top salary in the company, but top salary at that time wasn't a great deal. I made more money teaching fifth grade. However,

I did learn very quickly about profit sharing and such, and that helped.

Considering the fact that I really loved my work and wanted to continue, I flew to Denver prepared to continue working for E.C.A. but prepared to ask for and get a raise. I flew home to Massachusetts still working for the Company but without a raise. I was not happy. I began to feel that I was not appreciated, and that I was possibly even being used. Don't forget, I accepted the fact that the Company was in business, but I was in education, and I was in a family which needed financial support.

As luck would have it, *Learning Magazine* was just developing another aspect of their educational offerings. The Learning Institute, an educational consulting branch offering graduate credit to participants, was just being launched. I was invited to make an appointment, which I did, and flew three thousand miles to California for an interview. On my return to Massachusetts I was not empty handed. I had a contract, and I also had my freedom to accept private work, something E.C.A. never wanted their consultants to do.

When I joined the Learning Institute faculty, I worked on a summer team that first year. We traveled the country to various cooperating universities and taught courses. The team was made up of very knowledgeable educators who were strong powerful speakers in their respective fields. You had to know your area and be able to present it effectively, or you'd never survive. You had to have durability, or you'd get left behind. I loved meeting the new challenge.

After the summer courses were completed, I went on the hotel route as I had done for E.C.A., with one exception; I accepted fewer than one hundred days. Eventually, the Institute started to plan the programs of study for the upcoming summer. My instincts were good. I asked for and got my own team, and I suggested that

Phyllis be my partner. They knew of her background and trusted me, but it was still to my surprise that they said yes to everything.

That was the beginning of our traveling and teaching together on the road. It was time for us to work together. Phyllis had taught in an elementary school for twenty years. She had a good deal of experience in special programs and had already been teaching graduate courses in reading and literature. It was the natural thing for us to do. Between our classroom experience, our interest in and fantastic collection of children's books, and the knowledge of how to get books into the hands of kids and teachers, we were chomping on the bit to "hit the road."

Phyllis and I spent ten years helping to build the Learning Institute. We were allowed to choose our own team members and to pretty much call the shots within the realm of the Institute format. We met and worked with outstanding educators who helped us to share the love of reading with anyone who was willing to come and take from us. It was a wonderful ten year association with only minor and typical problems along the way. It was a growing experience, for it pushed us into new situations constantly.

When the Institute was sold to Springhouse Corporation of Pennsylvania, Phyllis and I knew it was time to leave. We knew we'd be giving up a position we had held and enjoyed for ten years, but we had other things to do. It was a good parting for us and, understandably, a bit sad, because we had worked long and hard with the Institute. At the same time there was great joy and excitement over the thoughts of forming our own company, taking another giant risk, and, best of all, having total freedom to direct our work. We were ready.

Shirley

I wonder if anyone really knows what it's like to earn a living as an in-service speaker in this country. It can be wonderful, but it can also be one of the most difficult jobs in the world. The next time you are made to go to an in-service presentation, please make the extra effort to be kind to the speaker—at least until you've heard the speech. It is very difficult to stand up alone in front of a whole school system. Please, put yourself in that speaker's place and give him a break.

I remember going to one school system for mandatory in-service at 3:30 on a Friday afternoon. When the superintendent introduced me the people booed. Then he walked by me and whispered, "Motivate them, Bill." Motivate them, hell! They're ready to attack. How would you like to stand in front of a mob like that?

After the session, and it wasn't one of my finest, I asked the superintendent how he got all these teachers to show up on a Friday afternoon. He said, "Well, we hold their pay checks." Under those conditions I'm not sure God would have been able to motivate them.

Another time I went to a small system for an in-service day. This time the superintendent got up in front of everyone and said, "I'm sick and tired of your gripes about in-service. Every year I offer you in-service programs, and every year you just gripe and gripe. If you don't like this guy, tell me, and we won't have any more in-service. Now, here he is." Need I say more?

Then there was the time when a principal got up in front of three hundred people to introduce me. He went on for ten minutes telling everyone of the wonderful and glorious things I had accomplished in my lifetime. I stood there listening. Suddenly I thought, "Wait a

minute. That's not me. I never did that." I knew that
the group probably didn't know just what I had done
throughout my career, so I just put on my humble
look and accepted all the compliments. After the ten
long minutes, the man finally turned to me and said,
"Please welcome Bill Martin, Jr., to North Dakota." I
said, "I'm not Bill Martin, Jr." He said, "Well, whoever
you are, just take it!" Then I thought, "If the group
doesn't like me I'll tell them I'm Bill Martin, Jr., and
if they do like me I'll tell them I'm Bill Halloran."
Thanks, Bill, I owe you one!

Every once in a while there's a little bit of revenge
associated with in-service. Please don't condemn me
for being into revenge. It comes with age. Some of you
know what I mean, and some of you will find out soon
enough. Besides, I like it.

Sometimes when you fly into an area for in-service
someone will pick you up at the airport and dump you
at the first Holiday Inn they come to. I've been dumped
at more Holiday Inns in this country than I'd like to
remember. I could write a book just about Holiday Inn
experiences. Of course, when in-service is over they
fight over who is going to take the speaker back to
the airport. "No, no, no. I'm not taking him back. You
brought him here, so you take him back," or, "No, I
did my share, now let someone else take him back." I
usually end up thumbing down the highway, dragging all the books behind me!

One time in late August I flew to Texas. It was a hot
Sunday afternoon, and I was dumped at a Holiday Inn,
as expected. I was to be the in-service speaker on Monday morning for hundreds of teachers in a large school
system. I found myself with nothing to do and just a
little bored, so I went to the room where you can relax
your muscles and shape up. No, not the gym and
sauna! I think some would call it a bar. I sat on

a bar stool and ordered a double coke on the rocks. After a while a young blonde woman came over and sat next to me. "Hi!" she said, "Hi, yourself," I answered. You have to understand that a "Hi" at my age is a real bonus in life. She followed with, "What's your name?" I said, "Bill. What's yours?" She told me her name was Shirley, and then she asked me what I did for a living. I never tell anyone what I do for a living. If you travel in this country and say you're an educator, everyone wants to tell you how to do your job. Everyone is an expert, and I'm sick and tired of all the experts who really don't know what they're talking about. Usually I say I work for Goodyear Tires. The next question is, "Do you have tires in all those cases?" to which I reply, "Just little ones." That will hold most people for a while.

Getting back to Shirley, I said, "How about you, Shirl? What do you do for a living?" She said, "Oh, Bill. Am I ever depressed." "Tell me about it, Shirl," I coaxed. She said, "I have to go to in-service for teachers tomorrow." When I heard that I just smiled and thought, "God is good. I'll fix Shirl." Our conversation continued. I asked, "Shirl, what does in-service mean?" She said, "We've got to go hear some guy talk about reading all day long." I offered, "Maybe he'll be good." She came back with, "They're never good. Believe me, they're never good." It was getting better by the minute. Then she said, "Do you know what a group of us are going to do while he's talking? We're going to sit in the back row and play cards." I said, "Shirl, that's rude." She said, "Who cares. He's going to be boring." "Okay, okay! Don't get hostile!" I finished my Coke and said, "Nice meeting you, Shirl. I've got to go now, but maybe our paths will cross again sometime."

The next morning I went to the auditorium. I was careful to keep my eye right on the door. The minute Shirley walked through the door I walked over and said, "Hi, Shirl." She was in shock. "What are you doing here?" she asked. I said, "I'm the boring speaker you're going to listen to all day today." Sheepishly, she asked, "What did I say about you last night?" I said, "You said a mouthful. Now sit right in the front row, and if you take those cards out I'll tell every person in the room just which bar we met in last night."

At break time Shirley came up to me and said, "Oh, Mr. Halloran, you're just wonderful." I said, "I know, Shirl. Sit down."

Another Survivor

I cannot look back on my traveling career without thinking of another consultant who has endured through the years and all the educational changes. Joe Wayman and I started working with educators at about the same time, and during these past fifteen years our roads have crossed hundreds of times and will probably cross a hundred more. It is written!

Joe has been out there, as I have been, doing in-service programs, parent groups, and going the Holiday Inn route facing joyful, as well as somber audiences. He has always survived, standing firmly on the philosophy that kids are very important and deserve the best from the educational system in this country. That children be allowed to develop their full potential in their own style and in their own way has always been uppermost in his message. Joe is one of the finest educators out there. I hope he will stay on the road for at least another decade or two and keep me company.

We were having lunch once when two very old men entered the restaurant with the help of their walkers. We both looked at each other and started to laugh. Almost simultaneously, we said, "That's us in a few years going to do in-service for some school system." Sometimes I'm overwhelmed by the fear that I'll be eighty years old someday standing in front of some group with my hair turning black, telling elephant jokes. Joe's fear is that he'll be eighty years old singing *"Mud, Mud, Mud"*, a song from one of his albums, to some group. In a strange way I hope both of our fears come true.

Because I've known Joe Wayman for so long and so

well, I could tell many wonderful, funny, and sad stories, but then the stories alone would fill a book. I'll leave that book for Joe to write and then share the royalties with me. I have decided to include one story, because it's one that I love to tell and one that involves three wonderful people.

I was in Houston working and staying at Joe's house a number of years ago. Joe has a beautiful home filled with all kinds of wonderful things from an original Rembrandt to a baby grand piano. As I went around looking at all the things he had collected over the years, he pointed out an unusual ceramic bull, which he had purchased in Mexico. He said, "Of all the things I own I love this bull the best." One thing led to another, and we found ourselves talking about gift giving, and he told me that he felt that when you give someone a gift it should be something you really treasure. It should be something you don't really want to give up. He said that when you do give up something of great sentimental value and feel the pain of that giving, then you know you've given a true gift. I felt that was very interesting, and I've never quite forgiven him for telling me about his feelings, because, now, gift giving is very difficult for me. No longer can I just go to a store and pick out perfume or a fountain pen. I'm always looking for the pain of giving one of my treasured possessions away. Joe ruined it for me, just as, I suspect, I am now ruining gift giving for some of you. Just think, we'll all be looking for the pain together.

Well, at Christmas time I received a package from Houston. Opening the package I found the ceramic bull from Mexico with a card that read, MERRY CHRISTMAS, BILL. I didn't have the heart to call and tell him that I really wanted the Rembrandt. Only kidding!

Joe was right when he said that true gift giving,

though joyful, has pain connected with it. I remember the first time I experienced the pain of gift giving for myself. Susan Jeffers, one of my very favorite illustrators, is a unique and very special person. I have always prided myself on having every book she has ever done. I even have a copy of *Buried Moon,* one of her very first books, which is now out of print. For me, it is a collector's item.

Upon showing Steven Kellogg my copy of *Buried Moon,* my collector's item, my one of a kind treasure, he said, "I'd love to have a copy of that book." I said, "It's out of print." He replied, "I know." The silence was deafening, and I was beginning to feel pain. Steven asked, "Do you have any idea of where I can get a copy?" I said, "No!" The pain was getting worse. In fact, it was quite unbearable. Quickly, I handed *Buried Moon* to Steven before I was totally consumed by agony, thinking to myself, "I'm going to kill Joe Wayman." I also discovered that along with the pain comes great joy. Knowing that Steven will treasure *Buried Moon* just as I did made the pain disappear. My treasure was in good hands.

I must add that several years later on the last day of Revival, an educational week at Fairfield University which I co-direct, I was speaking to the entire assembly of participants, when suddenly Susan Jeffers walked through the door and quietly took a seat. At the end of my speech she came up to me and said, "Bill, this is one of my first books. I'm sure you don't know it, but I'd like you to have a copy of *Buried Moon.*" What joy!

Over the years Phyllis and I had received many wonderful gifts from Joe, so I was always looking for a way to let him know how much we appreciated his thoughtfulness. When at Christmas time I read that Shirley Bassey was going to be at Korvettes in New

York City signing autographs, I decided that an autographed album would be just the thing for him. As far as pain goes, I wasn't sure there'd be any, but the album would still be special, because I knew that Shirley Bassey was a big favorite of Joe's.

When I got to New York, I thought, "This will be a snap. I'll just run over to Korvettes to buy the album and have it autographed." It just so happened that when I stepped out onto the street it was raining. "So what else is new?", I thought. But I was determined. Rain or no rain, I was going to get that album.

I got a real shock when I got to Korvettes. Hundreds of people were standing in a line that wrapped around the block. They were all waiting to get in to get an autographed album, too. I guess I thought I was just going to walk in, buy an album, have it signed, and walk out – ten minutes tops. Suddenly, I was facing a couple of hours in the pouring rain. I was beginning to feel a little pain.

Finally, I made it to the front door and my spirits were lifted. I remember thinking how it would soon be over and well worth the effort. It was like a bad toothache after the agony was over.

I'll never forget walking through the front door only to have my hopes dashed. I looked around carefully. Shirley was nowhere in sight. Then I heard someone say that she was on the sixth floor. I could hardly believe my ears. There were still hundreds of Shirley Bassey fans ahead of me. My pain suddenly became severe pain. But I was determined, because I knew that now it would be a true gift.

It took me almost three more hours to work my way up to the sixth floor. I was wet, cold, very angry, and racked with pain, when there I was standing in front of Shirley Bassey with album in hand. "What a gift this is going to be!" I thought.

Immediately I could see that Shirley had just about had it, too. She could hardly hold the pen in her hand as she tried to quickly scribble her name on each album. Well, I hadn't endured all those hardships for a scribbled name, no matter how much I understood her predicament.

When it was finally my turn, I smiled and politely said, "I would like you to write, 'To Joe Wayman—All my love, Shirley Bassey.'" Without looking up she replied, "I'm only signing my name." So, I replied in a very loud voice, "I've stood in line for hours. Now you write exactly what I tell you to write or you're going to see a wild, crazy man in front of you!" She looked at me in horror and quickly wrote, "To Joe Wayman —All my love, Shirley Bassey.'" In a very soft and gentle voice I said, "Thank you. I love your music," and calmly walked away. Shirley, wherever you are, I apologize. And I do love your music. It was a rare pleasure to sit in your audience sometime later and feel the electricity of your performance.

6. Lunch with Robert Newton Peck—"This time I had my suit, shirt and tie."

7. The pleasure of introducing Steven Kellogg

8. A quiet moment with Eric Carle

9. Robert Kraus, author of "Leo the Late Bloomer"—We finally meet.

10. Phyllis with Ina Tober and Pat McKissack—Friends, educators, authors.

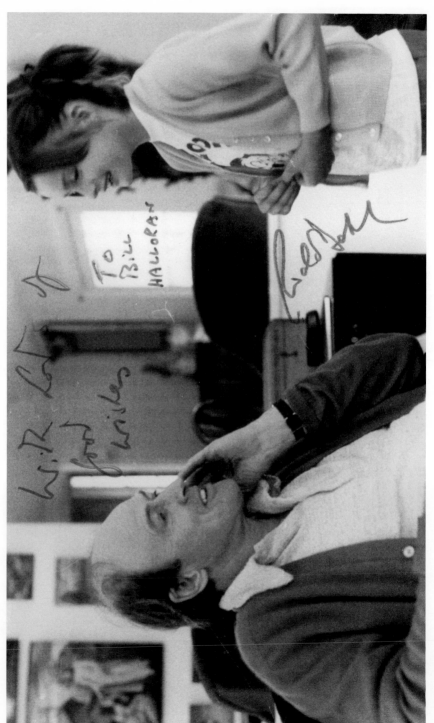

11. Roald Dahl with daughter, Lucy—"We met through letters and pictures."

12. Judy Blume—"Thanks for getting so many kids to read."

13. Joe Wayman—Author

14. Bill Martin, Jr.—Master teacher

15. "Have I got a book for you."

16. "Peter's Pocket" shirt.

17. The "can story"

18. "Spiderman will get kids to read."

19. "You've got to be kidding."

20. "Bringing kids and books together."

21. My book quilt—made by the children of Hopkins, Minnesota

22. "Stella"

23. Joanna Nicholson—Co-director of "Revival", an annual event for teachers.

24. Carl Tripp—Principal of Greenwood Park School.

25. Don and Linda Sass and Family—partners in Reading, Inc.

26. Beth

Burnout is Real

To this day I'm amazed that I never saw the warning signs of the particular kind of burnout that I experienced. Standing aside and looking back, I can clearly see how the years on the road could wear the strongest person down. It was a combination of things—always being in front of demanding audiences, always trying to motivate, always trying to meet everyone's needs, always trying to be at my best, always trying to get to the next city. Then there were all the receptions, chicken dinners, invitations to be with this group and that group, never ending questions, radio, newspaper and T.V. interviews. When added up, the sum was physical and emotional fatigue.

I really hadn't expected to pay a price for so vigorously pursuing the work I love. I mention this because I know full well that many of you think the sun shines on me twenty-four hours a day. In truth, the sun does shine on me, but occasionally clouds have passed over and have dimmed the light. In fun and with love, some of my best friends got together and actually gave me a black cloud, because I was always finding myself in some crazy situation. In short, the same clouds that settle over you in your classrooms, because of your dedication and your demanding work, manage to travel with me occasionally.

Many people sitting in front of me never stop to realize that I need as much, if not more, motivation as anyone. I can't help but think about Bette Midler when she sings about the lady walking down 42nd Street on a hot August day with a fried egg on her forehead. She asks the Lord to not let her walk down the street with a fried egg on her face. She tells how some people wear a fried egg on the outside, and some wear a fried egg on the inside—but we all wear a fried egg.

Suddenly my fried egg was in plain view. I think a thousand cities caught up with me at once. My world was heating up, and I was burning out. Before long, and with the thought in the back of my mind that I would make a terrible cranberry bouncer, along with the knowledge that I loved my work, I brushed off the fried egg. With the advice of Phyllis and dear friends who never intruded but suggested that I learn to be a little selfish with my time, I learned to gently say no, once in a while, to the constant barrage of offers that came.

The conditions for burnout vary with each job. Be on guard. Take care of yourselves, so that you can fully appreciate your chosen careers and bring enjoyment and contentment to your students and colleagues as you bring it to yourself. And don't ever kid yourself —education is a wonderful and exciting field but very demanding. Be good to yourselves!

My Prison Term

My relationship with Fairfield University was becoming stronger each year, and a big part of the reason was my friendship with Joanna Nicholson. I wish everyone could have a Joanna in their life. She is always pursuing one intellectual endeavor or another, and she knows how to communicate and play on all levels.

Joanna was in charge of special programs at Fairfield University for many years. She always encouraged me to go to the University to share my books and the love of reading. Because there was such trust and respect, if not always agreement, between us, Joanna was very receptive to my idea of trying something very special in education at the university. It would be something that had never been done before. I explained my idea by asking, "What do teachers need most?" Then I answered my question by telling her that they need renewal. They need to be revived, to be given a second, third, and fourth wind to recapture the joy and enthusiasm that somehow had drifted away from their teaching. The more I talked the more Joanna's head went up and down, slowly at first, then with vigor.

I knew it was right to suggest to her that we bring together, right at the University, the wonderful educators I had met along the way in my travels. Under one roof what an impact these people could have on the attitude and spirit of teachers, not to mention the effect they could have on curriculum content and, most importantly, on children. But my first and most important goal was to give teachers back their dignity if it were lost, their enthusiasm if it had fizzled, and their desire to go on if they had come to a dead end. At the very least it would be an experiential educational bonanza for those less needy.

In the summer of 1976, Fairfield University was the sight of the first annual Revival, the first educational offering of its kind anywhere in the United States. We just celebrated our tenth anniversary last year by bringing twenty-seven of the educational leaders in the country together to present lectures and workshops to eager teachers and administrators. We had to turn away over one hundred people for lack of space. Before the week was over people were trying to sign up again for number eleven. I suspect the next Revival is going to be our best—but then Joanna and I, who are the co-directors, say that ever year.

During Revival 1978 my career took an unexpected turn. As a result of that turn I have spent the last eight years in prison. Wait a minute!! Let me explain. It was Wednesday of Revival week when I received a call from Ina Tober asking me if I would go with her to the Maximum Security Prison in Somers, Connecticut to give a book talk. I was told that a group of men at the prison were trying to start a program dealing with children's books, but they didn't know very much about books and they needed help. Ina was willing to go, and she asked me to join her. We went to donate a few hours to a good cause. Little did we know that we would end up with a life sentence. Pardon the puns, but they're just writing themselves.

Ina and I drove to Somers Prison on that unbearably hot Wednesday afternoon in August. The excitement was building, for I had seen all those Humphrey Bogart movies. I could see in my mind a man with a raincoat over one shoulder, the fog rolling in, and a glamorous woman on his arm. It was "Bogie and Baby" headed for the "Big House." And there we were, a slightly older, slightly overweight "Bogie and Baby" headed for the "Big House." No fog, no raincoat, just a hot humid afternoon.

I had never been inside a prison before, and when we first entered the grounds and drove toward the main building I saw walls, guards and rifles. I remember saying, "Ina! I'm not going in there." She said, "Well, I am and I'm not going alone. Besides, you promised.", to which I replied, "You know I lie." All I could think of, once more, was "How the hell did I get myself into this one?"

I don't think there's any way I can adequately describe the feeling that suffuses your body when you hear the sound of metal doors and gates clanging shut behind you as you go deeper into the prison. How can I tell you what it felt like to walk among hundreds of inmates known only through novels and movies? How do I tell you of the eyes that stared with anger because the men behind those eyes did not want to be looked upon as animals in a zoo? How do I tell you exactly how I felt when I realized I was pushing a cart loaded with hundreds of kids' books down the main hallway of a prison? "Oh, Lord, why me?"

We walked down the endless hallway to the room where we were to meet the men who were interested in kids' books, of all things. We both knew it was nervous time. I hoped all the men were looking at Ina, and even then I couldn't think of one funny thing to say or one word of support for her. Finally, I said, "Ina, if these guys grab us, I'm going to offer them your body." "How could you do that?" she said. "Easy! You're a liberated woman. Everyone for himself."

Finally we reached our destination — none too soon. I think we were about to turn into screaming loonies. I immediately set out hundreds of books and was ready to begin. There were some men standing about the room in tan shirts and pants. Surely we didn't need that many guards to protect us. Impatiently I asked one of the guards when the prisoners were coming. He said, "What do you mean? We're the prisoners! Go ahead, mister. You can begin any time."

I think I must have appeared like a Don Knotts character as I nervously began my talk with a few elephant jokes (I always do—but can you believe it?), and the men just sat and stared. I tried a few more books, but still no response. Then I made a great little blunder. I was about to read *Alexander and the Terrible, Horrible, No Good, Very Bad Day* by Viorst—after all, it had worked that night with the group of emotionally needy people, so why not here?—when I heard myself saying, "Have any of you guys ever had a bad day?" I thought Ina was going to fall right out of her chair.

I believe in finishing what I start, so I kept on going as if I were in my fifth grade classroom. At that point I just wanted to finish and get the hell out of there. But then something wonderful began to happen. I was reading from Eloise Greenfield's poetry book, *Honey I love,* "I love. I love a lot of things, a whole lot of things. Like, my cousin comes to visit and you know he's from the South, cause every word he says just kind of slides right out of his mouth." Little by little I could feel the atmosphere of the room change. The men were listening and liking what they were hearing and seeing. When I was about to stop they said, "Keep going." They were just like my fifth graders. Then I realized they were just the same as the kids or anyone who loved their world. They were eager for the joy and excitement of learning. They were eager for a teacher to like them. They were eager for someone to try to understand or to care about them. They were eager for respect and trust. I was back in my classroom again, and it was an exhilarating feeling to witness the power of the coming together of people and books.

I spoke for about three hours that hot August afternoon. I left the prison that day a slightly different person. I knew I'd never be the same again. I had changed as a human being and as an educator. And my friend Ina was with me.

Returning to Revival was difficult, because I felt that every teacher should have been there to give witness to what had happened and to be touched by it. I knew I would not be capable of explaining the afternoon's events, so I didn't even try. I decided to pass it on through my teaching, my communicating, and my example.

After Revival I spent days buying children's books to take to the prison. I kept buying until my Visa exploded. But what an explosion!

To this day Ina and I go to the prison regularly and help in any way we can. The group of men, known as The Cabbage Patch (long before the dolls), changes from time to time, but all members of the group are involved in some phase of a radio broadcast for children about books. The program is heard throughout Connecticut. In addition, the men are involved in a writing program for children and produce an annual compilation of sample writings from children. The men of the Cabbage Patch have had a chance to share their experiences on several T.V. programs, too. I suspect that Ina and I will be a part of the Cabbage Patch forever.

The Women in My Life

Most of the women in my life have been very strong and have had a great influence on me. My mother is a strong, determined, and independent woman who will never end up in a rocking chair if she can help it. I pray for the same kind of perseverance and endurance. She lived through many crises and obstacles, as did many women of her generation. She survived the effects of the market crash, severe family illnesses, the raising of five active children—often alone because of my father's lengthy hospital confinements—boarders, dependent relatives, and she did it all with a good sense of humor. Such a woman does make a lasting impression.

Phyllis, of course, has been the major influence in my adult life and continues to give unswerving and unconditional encouragement, direction, and love to this day. It's good to have someone who understands my work and will give an honest opinion no matter how difficult it can be at times. We have achieved so very much together, the greatest accomplishment being our daughter, Beth.

There is Ina Tober, who came to teach third grade at Greenwood Park School and brought with her a breath of fresh air. She was not aware that she ministered to a jaded faculty with her humor, intelligence, humanism, and honesty. Her innate love of learning is infectious. As a friend, she is as tenacious as is humanly possible. She is that very rare kind of friend who is always there, never asking or intruding, but always ready to give. The love and affection that goes with her friendship is absolute. I feel that all children should be required to spend a year in her classroom, whether in first grade or in high school. Doors would open, especially the door to self-knowledge and acceptance. Fortunately, our daughter has been touched by Ina and her equally exceptional husband, Gerald, through our friendship, which I treasure more than words can express.

Joanna Nicholson has been a special person in my life for many years. You already know of the out of the ordinary person of whom I speak—Joanna, the risk-taker. Her counsel, support and loyalty have enriched my life. Talk about gusto! Whatever she tackles, from cooking to chairing a committee, she does with boundless energy and enthusiasm. She's an extraordinary communicator and an incredibly effective decision-maker. What I appreciate so very much is that she is not afraid to risk our friendship to be a friend. Joanna is my friend.

Then there came a woman called Pat McKissack, also known as Patricia or P.C., who allowed me to enter her world. It was a new world for me. Pat was the first black person in my life who let me get really close and ask all those questions that most of us find difficult to ask. If we're ever going to grow and change it must come from understanding, and there were things I didn't understand. I never personally knew a black person until I entered the service, and that's a whole other existence. With all due respect—Pat McKissack was my first black woman!

When I first met Pat she asked me why I didn't read any black poetry in my session. I replied that I had many black poetry books. She countered with, "That's a cop out. Not valid." So I told her that I didn't read any black poems because I didn't have black soul, and I didn't want to offend anyone. She gave one yell and laughed mercilessly. Finally, she said, "You certainly don't have black soul; you're the whitest man I've ever met. You obviously don't understand soul. Soul doesn't have a color. You have Irish soul. You have white soul. Don't ever be afraid to stand up there and read black poetry or black stories. You might not be able to do it the way it was intended, but Irish soul will be the second best way. People will love you for your Irish soul."

From that time on I've never let a session go by without reading black poetry. I just think of Pat McKissack and give it all the Irish soul I've got. Imagine how exciting it is to stand up and read her new book, *Flossie and the Fox,* with Irish soul. I suspect that Pat is going to be a major author of children's books. There is no one who has worked longer, harder, or is more deserving of the recognition, by way of her talent. Pat's not a talker, she's a doer. On second thought, she is a pretty good talker and a very dear and valued friend. Thank you, Pat, for my Irish soul!

Stella

There is no way for me to adequately describe Stella, but I'm going to try, in the hope that my effort will enrich lives and perpetuate the memory of my colleague, my partner, my friend.

In a strangely quiet way, Stella ruled the whole school. The principal, teachers, kids, secretary, and custodian were under her spell. You must admit that if you rule the secretary and the custodian you really do have power. Today the custodian—tomorrow the world! Personally, I'd rather tangle with the superintendent than with the secretary or custodian. Anyway, Stella was undisputedly in charge. With one look she could pin you to the wall. She was a no nonsense lady and not to be trifled with. She was stern and demanding, yet loving and giving—always there for anyone who needed her. She was respected for her strong convictions and for her loyalty. She was special.

My feelings for Stella came to the surface from the moment I first laid eyes on her. Oh, Lord, I was afraid of her, and that fear lasted my whole first year of teaching. I never crossed her. Not once!! The amazing thing is that the kids weren't afraid of her at all. They flocked to her classroom, arriving early and staying late. And believe me, she ran a tight ship.

I should have recognized it right away, but it took me awhile to figure out the source of the magic she held for the kids. It was really quite simple; she loved all of them—a lot—and they knew it. She never played favorites, and that's not easy to do. If she had a favorite, no one ever knew, and she never told.

Also, Stella was very close to nature, and she brought that appreciation and respect right into her classroom.

The kids responded strongly to such a love of animals and plants, as did everyone in the area. Most people knew that Stella loved birds. For miles around, anyone who had a sick bird or found an injured bird brought it to Stella, and she would nurse the bird back to health. She seldom lost a bird.

In the spring when the baby birds would occasionally fall out of their nests, Stella would take care of them until they were strong enough to fly. Sometimes she would be nursing a dozen birds, all in separate cages, at the same time. She'd get up every two hours during the night to feed them all with a tiny eye dropper. Then she'd drag all the birds in their cages to school every day and teach the children about them and how to care for them. God help you if you happened to arrive or leave at the same time as Stella. She'd have you dragging bird cages back and forth for hours.

Now, I like birds—at a distance. I never had any great desire to have birds around me all day. To tell you the truth, none of the faculty loved the birds, but no one would dare say that to Stella. For years I put up with the feathered creatures and never said a word.

It was inevitable that the day would come when I could no longer keep my feelings in. Our rooms were separated by a moveable wall, and Stella had the controls on her side, of course. Do you realize what that meant? I had no control of the wall. She opened and closed it at will. That wall would fly open without a moment's notice, and I'd hear something like, "Take my class! I'm going for coffee." I was usually as mad as hell when I answered, "Yes, Stella." If I ever find myself looking for another classroom job, my first question in the interview will be, "Are there wall controls, and do I get them?"

You have to consider the situation I was in. It was difficult not to be able to speak out, always having to keep my cool. It was especially difficult when all the birds were nursed back to health, because she'd let them fly around free in the classroom. Then she would open the wall and go for coffee. I know. I can hear you moaning. Those damn birds were dive-bombing all through my lessons. The kids loved it. You try living with that for a while and see if you don't turn into a pressure cooker.

So, one year Stella had a huge grackle in her room flying free. She said it was a grackle. I say it was an eagle. You never knew where the damn thing was. You had to teach with one eye on the move at all times. The day finally came when I reached the breaking point. The wall was open, Stella was at her desk, and I was teaching her group and mine when all of a sudden that eagle of a bird flew over my head and shit in my hair. I really lost it! Before I knew what I was doing I heard a voice yelling, "That's it, Stella. I've had it with your birds, especially this eagle. I'm going to kill the damn things!" Very calmly Stella got up from her desk, walked over to me, looked me in the eye, and rubbed the shit into my hair saying, "Your hair's white; the bird shit is white. If I just rub it in no one will know the difference. Now quiet down and teach the lesson." After a few seconds of silence, I heard another voice say, "Yes, Stella." The kids cheered with joy, and I finished the lesson. Privately, I still plotted to kill that thing.

Then there was the time we were having parent conferences. Stella and I always held our meetings with parents together because we shared most of the kids. We were sitting at a table in the back of the room and Mrs. _____ walked in for her conference. Mrs. _____ was wealthy and was draped in furs and jewels. Her hair was perfectly styled with every strand in place. She sat down, in all her splendor, with her back facing the room. Now, Mrs. _____ was unaware of the eagle loose in the room, and I was not about to tell her. All of a sudden, right in the middle of the conference, I looked up and saw the eagle coming at Mrs. _____ full force with claws out ready to perch. It landed with a thud! There sat Mrs. _____ with a huge bird on her head. I thought she was going to have a heart attack. I thought I was going to have a heart attack.

Mrs. _____'s face went white. She sat like a zombie, unable to utter a sound. Then Stella said, "What's the matter, Mrs. _____? Don't you like birds?" The woman got up, turned, and walked out. We never saw her again for the rest of the year. To this day I wonder how we ever escaped going to jail or being fired.

There were just so many things that happened over the years. Like the time Carl came to us and said he needed certain records filled out right away. "Well," I thought, "there goes that lesson." Stella and I opened the wall, gave the kids an assignment, and sat at Stella's desk working on the records. Stella's top drawer was open as we sat there working. The room was very quiet until all of a sudden Stella slammed the top desk drawer closed and gave out a scream that could be heard in China. The kids and I were in shock. Still screaming, she began to cry. I kept saying, "What's the matter, Stel? What's the matter?" When she finally was able to take a breath she just looked at me and yelled, "I slammed my boob in the drawer!" She got up and ran out of the room, and there I was with fifty kids upset and asking, "What did she do?" What could I say? I told them the truth. Very matter-of-factly, I said, "She shut the desk drawer on her boob." To my amazement, some of the kids said, "Oh," and went back to work.

When Stella finally came back to the room she looked me in the eye and said, "I don't want to hear one word from you, and you better not say a word in the teacher's room, either. Do you understand me?" "Yes, Stella."

Through the years I have talked about Stella in my lectures, and it has now gotten to the point where people raise their hands and ask me to tell a "Stella story." People tell me they brought a friend with them just to hear about Stella. I think she has so much appeal, because we can all relate to her in one way or another. She's so real.

Once Stella asked me to stop telling all those stories about her. I said, "But Stel, they're all true." She said, "I know, but you don't have to tell the world." Then I said, "Stella, I have made you famous all over the country." That's when she smiled, as only she could, and said, "I know."

For the last few years of our partnership, Stella had been talking about retiring. Every time she brought up the subject I would get her not to leave. I told her I would never be able to find another partner like her, and that, although we were like night and day, we were meant for each other. I would always tell her that we would leave together. I would find a new job, and she could retire. I just felt that I didn't want to stay there without her. Our relationship was that special. She would always end up saying, "You're right, Bill, we'll leave together. That's the way it should be."

As fate would have it, my life changed without much warning. At the end of the summer of 1974 I quit my job and went on the road for E.C.A. Everything was such a whirlwind experience, and my new job, with all the traveling, left me exhausted. I really hadn't seen anyone or gone anywhere for a few months while I was getting accustomed to my new schedule.

It was holiday time, and I was home for a few weeks determined to catch up on everyone and everything. My phone rang, and a soft gentle voice said, "Bill, this is Stella." I said, "Oh, Stella. I'm so glad to hear from you. I've been wanting to talk with you and tell you just why I decided to quit." She said, "Bill, I just want to say Merry Christmas, you son-of-a-bitch," and she hung up.

And then there was Stella's retirement party. Carl called me and asked if I would go and roast Stella as a little surprise for her. I said, "Are you kidding? Stella would kill me. If you think it would be fun, why don't you do it?" "Bill, you're the only one who could really do the job right," he pleaded. I knew what he meant. I also knew I'd be placing my life in jeopardy.

Of course I agreed to roast Stella, but it was against my better judgment. The big night finally arrived, and there was a wonderful turnout for this special lady, just as I knew there would be. Everyone would go all out for Stella. Toward the end of the meal, Carl announced that Stella was going to be roasted. That was my cue to stand up. When Stella saw me stand up she also stood up, pointed a finger at me and said, "Don't you dare." I mustered up all my courage, took a deep breath, and said, "Stella, sit down and keep quiet. Tonight is my night. It's my time to even the score and let the chips fall where they may." You could hear a pin drop in the room. You see, no one ever talked back to Stella that way. The anticipation and the love in the room was high, for everyone realized it would be a once in a lifetime happening.

Believe me, I told it all from the birds to her boob in the drawer. But I saved the best one until the end, when I was sure she thought I was through. I knew my last story would crack the already thin ice under my feet, but I didn't care. I really didn't know how she'd take it, but I had gone this far so why not finish the job—and maybe myself in the process.

From the very beginning of my career I was not a

checker. Some teachers spend their whole day putting little check marks in a million little squares. I couldn't stand all those little marks and squares. I refused to be a checker for the system. I wanted to teach and not check. I was determined to never fall into the checking trap. You guessed it! Stella was a checker of the highest order. She had a check sheet for everything. I even think she had check sheets in her car and checked her way home.

The first month of my teaching career the coach came to me and issued me all the sports equipment for my room for the year. He gave me the hoops, the loops, the ropes, the bats, the balls, etc. He also gave me a check sheet and told me that at the beginning of recess I should check out all the equipment and at the end of recess check it all back in. That way, he reasoned, I wouldn't lose track of anything. That first week I sat by the door every recess period with my check sheet. Check-it-out, check-it-in, check-it-out, check-it-in, check-it-out, check-it-in. Those kids and that check sheet were driving me crazy. The kids changed their minds every two seconds.

By the end of the first week I was about out of my mind, not being a checker by nature. I knew I had to do something fast, or I'd never survive. Besides, I was missing my coffee break because of all the damn checking. All of a sudden it dawned on me. I had the perfect solution. I wondered why I hadn't thought of it sooner. After all, I was supposed to be encouraging responsibility.

Monday morning at recess time I called the kids around me and said, "Do you see this check sheet? Watch me. I'm going to rip it up. Do you see this equipment? It's very expensive, but it's for you to enjoy. Take care of it because when it's gone, it's gone. Now, take the equipment and go play."

In one week that wonderful equipment was all gone. Most of it was on the roof, and I was in the teacher's room where I was supposed to be, having coffee.

Remember, Stella was a checker. So one day I went to her and told her to come down and have coffee with me. I reminded her that she never gets to the teacher's room any more. She glared at me and said, "How do you do your checking and have time to get to the teacher's room?" I said, "Stella, listen to me. Trust me. If you do exactly what I tell you you'll be in the teacher's room drinking coffee in five short days. Just rip up that check sheet and tell the kids when the equipment is gone, it's gone. In five short days it will be gone. It'll all be on the roof with my stuff." She gave me, the new kid on the block, a look that told me to take myself and my weird ideas and get away.

I left, never thinking she'd ever take my advice. To my surprise, on Friday Stella waltzed into the teacher's room and said, "Bill, it worked. All my stuff is on the roof with yours. It's really quite wonderful. I don't know why I didn't think of it years ago. We'll always be able to have coffee together now." I quickly suggested that we be quiet about the whole thing. I suggested we not tell the other teachers, reminding her that the roof wasn't big enough. So we went with that plan for five long years. The first week of school the coach would give us the equipment and check sheet. "Thank you," we'd say politely, rip up the sheet and give the kids the equipment. On schedule, in five days we'd be having coffee in the teacher's room.

After a few years, the kids knew exactly what to do. They'd just go out and throw the stuff on the roof. No, no! I'm just kidding. But something was happening, because by the fifth year we got rid of the stuff in just three short days. Stella was actually out on the playground throwing the stuff on the roof herself. I said,

"For heaven's sake, Stella, can't you be a little more discrete?" "I need coffee," she yelled.

But our sixth year the tide turned on us. We got a new coach with new ideas and new policies. The new coach was going to revolutionize our school. Unfortunately for him, the new coach had never met the likes of Stella.

We were issued the equipment, as usual, and the check sheet. Still, we gave the equipment to the kids to get rid of it just as before. By Friday we were having coffee, as expected. It was the same old routine. New coach, my eye. He would be just like the old coach. We had nothing to be concerned about if we just kept quiet.

Then I took my kids down to meet the new coach. "New Coach—my kids. Kids—meet New Coach." The first words out of New Coach's mouth were, "Kids, I've issued all your equipment. Is there anything else I can get for you?" In good sporting fashion the kids said, "Mr. Halloran says when it's gone, it's gone, and it's already gone—on the roof." Mr. New Coach eyeballed me, I eyeballed him right back. Who is this guy to tell an old time teacher how to do it? I stood my ground. But then Mr. New Coach hauled me into the principal's office, and I got chewed out up one wall and down the other. I hardly knew what to say, so I said, "Well, Stella doesn't have her equipment either." I figured we were partners in everything. They hauled her into the office and chewed her out, too. She came at me ready to kill. I said, "Stella, we're partners. We have to face this together. You didn't complain for five years during the good times. It just so happens that now we have fallen on bad times, and it's important that we stick together and ride out the storm."

Shortly after that incident we were issued new equipment and, yes, new check sheets. We were ordered back to our rooms and to start checking. There we were, day after day. Check-it-in, check-it-out, check-it-in, check-it-out. On Thursday my door opened and in walked Stella. She said, "Where are you?" "What do you mean?" I asked. "You're not down having coffee," she said. "Are you kidding?" I said, "I'm checking everything. Aren't you?" "Oh, Bill," she said, "I told my kids when it's gone, it's gone. All my stuff is on the roof again." "Stella," I yelled, "I don't believe you. They're going to kill you." Then she asked for half of my stuff. I said, "No way!" Then she asked, "Aren't we partners anymore?" "Not any more," I said. "This stuff belongs to me. Now, please excuse me. I have to do my checking." Check-it-in, check-it-out, check-it-in, check-it-out.

Then it happened, and I'll never forget it. I was teaching math—fractions. I was standing in the back of the room. Stella must have been in the teacher's room, and they must have hit her and hit her hard over the equipment situation. When you hit Stella, Stella hits the school. She must have come flying down the hall with flames trailing behind her. Suddenly, Stella was at my door screaming across the room, "Mr. Halloran, have you checked your balls today?" I couldn't believe what I was hearing. The kids looked at me. The kids looked at her. I looked at me. I looked at her. Then I made my mistake by saying, "What did you say?" A little kid yelled out, "She wants to know if you checked your balls today." I started to laugh, and when I broke into a full laugh she caught on. She got angry and yelled, "Do you have to make a joke out of everything I say?" Then she slammed the door in my face. Hell! I hadn't even said anything. And you know that thirty kids went home that day and said that Mrs. _____ asked him if he checked his balls today. And you know thirty mothers asked, "What did he say?"

When the laughter died down the group all turned to look at Stella, who was back at the door. Her face was stern, and her eyes were staring right at me. Slowly she walked toward me. The room was silent, and my heart was pounding. I thought, "Oh, please, don't hit." She walked right up to me, looked me in the eye, took my face in her hands, and said, "I love you." And with that, Stella was roasted.

Before I move on, I have to tell you one more Stella story. I made her famous all over the country with this one, but I think I also lost my reputation as a reading consultant.

More often than not, people will come up to me before I'm about to give a speech and ask me if I'm going to tell this particular story. If I should forget to tell it and time starts to run out, someone will always interrupt me in the middle of a sentence and ask, "Aren't you going to tell the 'Stella Story?'" This is the one they're asking for.

Teachers are always asking me about using films with the kids, and I always smile when I hear the word film. If you're a normal teacher, normal—not whacked out—and you hear the word "film," what shoots through your mind? Will that film fit into my curriculum? Hell, no! Will that film be on my grade level? Hell, no. If you're normal, you'll think one thing and one thing only; how big is the can? If you don't know what I'm talking about you're a weirdo or you haven't been there long enough. The bigger the can the happier the teacher. A forty minute can is everything in life to a teacher trying to hang on.

With regard to films—what did they teach us in college? What was the never to be broken rule? Don't ever, ever show the kids a film unless you have previewed it first. Well, forget all that nonsense. My first year out I did everything I had been told to do when I was in college. I gave up my lunch hour to preview films and write pre and post questions. Did you hear me? I gave up my lunch hour. But the second year out I said, "Give me that can. Give-it-to-me!" I'd run it forward, backward, and sideways. "Hey, kids. Do you want to see how it looks forty minutes backwards?" Oh, stop your moaning, teachers. Kids love to see films backwards, especially films on fractions. How many of you have ever put your thumb on the reel to slow it down a little? Oh, come on. Some of you have deep scars in your thumbs. I'll bet some of you don't even have thumbs anymore.

Getting back to the story, It was a Friday afternoon, and I had a can. It was a big can. It was the biggest can I had ever seen in my life. Anytime I had a can, all I had to do was quietly go next door to Stella's room and hold up the can. Like magic that wall would fly open. You never had to ask Stella twice! But Stella had the flu this particular day, and she wouldn't go home. She stayed and gave us all the flu. She was dedicated. So I said, "Stella, go on down to the teacher's room, and I'll take the kids. The can is good for forty minutes, fifty if I put my thumb on the real." She went. Wouldn't you? How many times does an offer like that come along? You learn to take such an offer before someone changes their mind.

Then I got to thinking about it. "It's Friday afternoon. I should be a good guy and help my colleagues," I thought. So I very quietly went across the hall to the two third grade teachers. Very quietly I opened their doors, and very quietly I held up the can. They came flying across the hall like bullets—like bullets! They never asked for the grade level, topic, or anything. Who the hell cared. All they ever asked was, "How big is your can?"

Now it seemed as though I had a thousand kids in my room. It was wall to wall kids, three teachers, the projector, and the can. We were ready to settle in for the

Friday afternoon film fest. And that's called—making it to Saturday. We were ready, and three teachers uttered those magical words that only normal educators really understand—"ROLL'EM!"

Let me tell you, a thousand kids and three teachers will never forget what happened that day. It turned out to be one of the more memorable learning experiences. The title of the film was *The Intruder.* I had selected it. You better believe it. That's one committee I volunteered to be chairman of. I was in charge of "the can committee." You can have the Sunshine Fund. I'll take care of can selection, and I'll help get us through the year.

I just knew the film was good for all age levels. I just knew it. After all, it had an R for recommend. We put that can on, and we let 'em roll. Three teachers sat back to be saved on a Friday afternoon. Do you know the feeling? It wasn't bad in the beginning. It was teaching the kids not to let strangers come in to your house late at night. Even if they say they have a flat tire and want to use the phone. It told them to speak through a closed door and ask for a number to call to be helpful but to definitely not open the door. Not bad. Not bad. The kids were really into it.

I turned to give the other two teachers the high sign. Their heads were bobbing. Isn't it amazing how the minute the lights go out and the film goes on all teachers go right to sleep. Go by any classroom where a film is being shown, and you'll see the teachers slumped in their chairs in the back of the room. Their heads never come up until they hit on the chair in front. Then the heads fly up, and there's a groove on the forehead for a week. Now you have a groove on the forehead and a groove on the thumb. You can always tell just who shows the most number of films by the depth of the grooves. You'll even hear some teachers saying, "Yup, these are my movie grooves."

Suddenly, all was not moving along smoothly. The dangerous stranger came to mother's door and rang the bell. Mother opened the door, and mother was only wearing a flimsy robe. I thought, "Oh, my. No, Bill, this is a film for kids. Get those thoughts out of your mind." But then mother said, "Come on in." I thought, "Mother, what the hell are you doing?" Now we were in the living room with mother, her two kids, and the dangerous stranger. A thousand eyeballs were glued to the screen. Three teacher's eyeballs were glued to the screen. No one was sleeping anymore.

All of a sudden, the dangerous stranger whipped out a pistol and said, "Into the bedroom." The other two teachers looked at me, and I gave them a don't-worry-trust-me kind of look. Then the stranger said, "Up against the wall." I thought, "Oh, no, please. My job!" Then the man headed toward Mother with his hand aimed at her breast. You could hear a pin drop. Well, I jumped up, grabbed that projector, turned that thing off, and a thousand kids screamed, "Don't, don't! Don't turn it off." "I told you kids that if I heard one more sound in this room I'd shut that thing off!!!" I said. Well, what would you have said?

Stella walked in at this moment and said, "Bill, what the hell are you doing?" I quickly explained, and she said, "Don't worry. I'll take care of everything." She got the kids all into their seats and started to explain the situation. "Children, the dangerous stranger was just searching Mother for her jewels," she said. At that, I jumped up and yelled, "Recess!" Then I turned to Stella and said, "Are you trying to get us all fired?" I thought she was going to kill me on the spot.

We didn't show any films for a while after that. We just prayed that the kids hadn't gone home and told their parents about the dangerous stranger searching

Mother for her jewels.

For years I've been telling the "can story", and for years people have been laughing and begging me to tell it again and again. It was in Florida during a workshop presentation I was giving when a woman stood up and said, "I have to tell you something. I heard you speak a few years ago, and I taped your presentation including the "can story." Some time ago I went to the hospital, because I had been diagnosed as having cancer. I remember feeling so afraid that I would never be leaving the hospital. All kinds of thoughts were running through my mind, and I thought of you. I thought of your joy and your wonderful ability to make people laugh and cry. I thought of how you make people feel things they never felt before. I told my husband to get the tapes of that wonderful crazy man and bring them here to me. I played the "can story" over and over, and you made me laugh until it hurt. Bill, I'm here today because of you and that story. Thank you and don't ever stop telling about that can that saved my life."

I didn't get to see Stella very often after I left the classroom, but we were close friends. We both knew it. Time and distance didn't matter. We had a special relationship, and we had shared some of the most wonderful experiences of our careers.

A few years later when I learned that Stella had entered the hospital and that her situation was very serious, I knew I had to see her. I had to go and say good-bye, and I had to go alone. It wasn't easy walking into her hospital room. The minute I got there she said in her stern voice, "I've been waiting for you." "I know," I replied. After a few uneasy moments she asked me to tell her some funny stories. I thought to myself, "I can't tell you funny stories, Stella. I've come to say good-bye. Not today, Stella, not today." But slowly we started talking, and before I knew it I was telling stories, and we both began to laugh and laugh. Then I did it all—birds, bird shit, Mrs. _____ at the parent conference, boobs in the drawer, check-it-in, check-it-out, and, of course, the big can. We talked and laughed all afternoon. We never spoke of her illness, but at the end of my visit we hugged each other tightly for a long time. We both knew it was good-bye.

Shortly after, I stood at her grave side and realized a part of my life had ended. A great sadness came over me. Then I looked at David, her young grandson, who was holding a dozen colorful balloons. He passed them out, and we let them fly into the air. I knew Stella was somewhere smiling. Then I began to smile, for I realized that I would be telling "Stella Stories" the rest of my life. I realized that our relationship would continue, in a different way, forever.

Part Four
Some Things To Think About

The Gray Group

There's a group of kids in our country that I call the "gray kids." These are the kids that will never be the A students nor the F students. They go through school never being in the limelight. Teachers never give them much attention. They are usually quiet, though not necessarily shy, and accustomed to not being noticed. They're not neglected, in the strict sense of the word, but they are neglected in a way that encourages them to blend in with the woodwork, so to speak.

There will never be large sums of money appropriated for the gray kids. The money always goes to both extremes, and these poor kids are caught in between. They're a little like the middle ground of the tax scale. Help usually reaches the very wealthy or the very poor. We're not intentionally mean to these kids, but we just don't see them clearly. Consequently, we don't seem to have a lot of time for them.

The gray kids are in every classroom every year, and I think it's time we recognized them. We will find in this group some of the brightest and most creative students who simply do not know how or care to fight their way out. Perhaps they have found a comfortable little niche for themselves and are content not to be more aggressive or the shining stars in our schools. They remain unnoticed because they are the kids who do as they are told, never cause problems, and never complain. They don't have a label yet. Feeling the way I do about labels, it might be the one thing they have in their favor. However, I do think we must recognize and label, if necessary, these kids, so we can start to bring out their hidden colors. More importantly, we must help them to want to explore all their colors. A line from one of Shel Silverstein's books comes to mind—"And all the colors I am inside have not been invented yet."

I am confident that some of you really don't know what I'm talking about because you sailed through school and everything was rosy, just as I am confident that some of you know exactly what I am saying. I'm sure a few of you are feeling some pain right now because you're remembering that it was hell growing up in the gray group. You might not even want to go on reading about it, because all that hurt is coming to the surface again. You must read about it, and think about it, and do something about seeing that it doesn't go on.

Perhaps the best way to describe kids who experience the color gray is by calling attention to the fact that there are people in the world who die a little inside when they hear someone say, "Don't you miss the good old school days? Weren't they some of the best days of our lives?" And these people think to themselves, "They weren't the good old days for me. I can hardly bear to think of them." Watch carefully the next time you're in a group, and you hear similar words. You'll recognize the person who was in the gray group. Chances are, that person is still in the gray group, although many come upon people and situations that help to pull them up and out.

I was teaching a five day summer course a few years ago, and I remember picking on a young teacher in my audience. Every time I picked on her she just glowed, which gave me the signal that it was all right to tease her a little. I always seem to pick on someone, because it helps us all to laugh a little, to have some fun at no one's expense, and to make it through the day. So, for five days this young teacher was my target, and for five days she just glowed.

When the course was over on that last day, I was in the meeting room alone packing up my books when the door opened and in walked my young friend. She quietly asked, "Can I talk to you?" For a moment I thought, "Oh, dear! I went too far. I teased her too much. I stepped over the line." That line is so very delicate for me in my classroom, just as it is for you in your classroom. We all step over that line from time to time. The only thing we can do is to try to step back and hope we didn't do any lasting damage, and, of course, try to be more sensitive. The young woman started to speak. She said, "I want to tell you something." With those words, tears started to well up in her eyes. She continued, "You talked about the gray group today. I have spent my whole life in the gray group. You're the only teacher who ever picked me out and made me feel special. Thank you." I was back in my fifth grade classroom. The girl left that afternoon with a special feeling because her teacher noticed her.

I hope you will not pass through this section of this book too lightly. You must understand that there is a large gray group in this country, and it seems to be getting larger every year as class sizes grow and teachers' burdens get heavier. Please join forces with me to eliminate this group and give these kids the little bit—that's all it requires—of help and a chance to get the attention and recognition that they deserve. Tomorrow will be without some of its best thinkers, and doers, and leaders if we do not do something to help these gray kids today. Think about the gray kids, and talk about the gray kids with your colleagues. We're capable of making a big difference in the lives of these kids, and we can't go on ignoring that fact or these kids. Consider the signs painted. Now let's get the march going.

Building a Foundation

Presently, the whole country is talking writing, pushing writing, and buying into writing programs. I think this is happening because we have suddenly discovered that our kids can hardly write a simple sentence, even if they have some thoughts they want to express. What else can we expect when so many of our kids were brought up on filling in blanks, putting an X in a box, or circling a word? The kids have been deprived of hearing the language. The beautiful words and the flow of the language is not in their heads and hearts. So now, the push is on to get the kids writing successfully.

I'm disturbed over the fact that in some instances we are building our house without a foundation, and without a solid foundation our house will soon collapse. The skills side of writing does not create a foundation for writing; rather it supports the structure. Just as in reading, the skills are an aid to reading—they are not reading. If you asked a child to tell you what reading is, would you want that child to reply that phonics is reading? Would you want any child to believe that punctuation is writing?

The only solid foundation for a writing program is a literature program. A very important part of the literature program is a read-aloud program. Why is it so difficult for us to accept this knowledge that should be obvious to us? Our common sense and observation should make this perfectly clear to us. To be able to write successfully, our children must hear and feel the flow of the language, be rich in vocabulary, and have many experiences with which to react to ideas. One simple way to ensure that the children have all these necessary elements is through literature.

Children need to read, to listen, to discuss, and to debate. Some children will never be able to travel far, never experience the outer limits of their world, but the literature can bring their world to them through rich vocabulary and the experiences of others. We, as teachers and parents, must give our children all of this through the magic of books, or our children will remain static.

Travel around the country with me, and you'll be in shock when you realize how few schools promote a real literature program—even for the very young. Reading to kids stops so early in life, when it should last forever. Somewhere around second grade we stop reading to our kids for a variety of reasons, such as not having enough time or believing that the kids should read for themselves for practice. Certainly children need to practice their new skills, but that doesn't mean that the need for reading aloud is diminished. In fact, because learning to read is so difficult and painful for so many kids, it's important for them to have continuous positive experiences with books, so they will never turn away. If we go on much longer, the first grade teachers will be saying, "Reading to kids is a job for the kindergarten teacher."

Every day I hear the same old story: "I'd like to read to the kids, but I just don't have time." We don't have time to build our houses carefully so they will not collapse on us. We don't have time to build our houses with the best possible materials so we will not have to put unbelievable amounts of time and money into repairs.

When searching out a good writing program, or when attending a workshop or course on writing, if literature is left out—BEWARE!! I can't imagine promoting writing without promoting reading, and, in particular, read-aloud. Unfortunately, some of the people who have moved into the field of writing because it's "in" give themselves away when they do not recognize and promote the need for a good reading program on which to build a writing program.

I am appalled by administrators who come down hard on their teachers for reading to kids, especially in the upper grades. They say it's a waste of time, but these same administrators go all out for writing, in those same upper elementary and middle school grades. They don't understand that, because of their lack of understanding of the relationship between reading and writing, they are building on a weak foundation.

A sequential literature read-aloud program and writing program go hand in hand. It cannot be hit or miss. When we reach an understanding of the fact that we need a total language program based on listening, speaking, reading and writing, then we will turn out a nation of readers and writers.

Book Reports

Why do we insist that our kids write a book report once a week? If the answer to this question has anything to do with helping kids to be better readers or to encourage kids to read—it isn't working!

There are far less painful ways of teaching main character, plot, mood, etc. than through a traditional book report. As a matter of fact, if parents at home and all primary teachers simply and casually discuss the elements of a story as they read together daily, it would be so natural for the same elements to be recognized in more sophisticated reading material in the higher grades. It would probably be a pleasure, a sought after assignment, to personally choose a novel and do a report on it when a child loves to read in the first place. Common sense should tell us that our first and most important task is to instill in our kids a desire to read. We must motivate the kids and then sustain that motivation.

Asking children to do a weekly book report is not going to inspire or motivate anyone to read. If anything, such an assignment would probably associate reading with a negative experience. All too often, kids are made to write book reports before the ground work has been done. It's a little like asking the kids to do a complicated mathematical problem before they learn simple sums and differences. And when a child knows how to write a good solid book report, but is made to write one weekly, it is like asking a child who already knows how to do long division to do one hundred examples nightly. It's a waste of time, it's boring, and it detracts from the joy that should be associated with learning and growing.

Book reports do not create enthusiastic readers, just as phonics does not create enthusiastic readers. Each can aid the reading process if handled thoughtfully, carefully, and with an understanding of its place of importance in the scheme of things.

Readers are created by exposure to books at an early age with no pressure applied, such as in a consistent read-aloud program strictly for enjoyment. Readers are created when a child brings personal experiences to the ideas of authors and has an opportunity to discuss reactions. Readers are created when children have access to a variety of good literature and the freedom to pick and choose with gentle guidance rather than interference.

Please, I beg of you, stop the weekly book reports. Do you know how many parents sit at kitchen tables night after night yelling at their kids who are already frustrated enough and don't need any more pressure? Do you know how many kids and parents go to bed crying over some foolish book report that means nothing in their lives? Then we wonder why our children don't like to read.

Some of the sweetest words I ever heard in my classroom were, "Mr. Halloran, I loved this book. Can I tell you about it? What did you think about the part....? Do you have another one just like it?" Those words told me that I did my teaching. Most of my kids loved to read book after book after book. That's what I was after, and no weekly book report could accomplish that for me. Teaching plot, mood, etc. was a snap because the most important ingredient was there—the desire to read.

When a child loves a book so much and wants another just like it, do you know the problem the teacher faces? It's finding another **just like it**. And that means **just like it.** This is where Nancy Drew and the Hardy Boys come in. Every book is just like the last one and that's all right, but some educators have banned Nancy with each new decade. Nancy Drew is not good literature? She'll warp the minds of our young? Nancy is dull, blah, boring, and doesn't have enough energy to warp my mind, good literature or not. As a matter of fact, Nancy is aging, and I wish she'd go have an affair with one of the Hardy Boys before it's too late—and it doesn't matter which one. Nobody, including Nancy, would know the difference.

Most of my generation read all the *Nancy Drew* books, *The Hardy Boys, The Bobsy Twins*, and of course, *Five Little Peppers and How they Grew*. Every time we read one of these books we practiced our reading skills and became better readers. Do you really think minds can be warped by such books when there is a good literature foundation already in place? Kids who read horse stories for a solid year are not hurt by their choice and eventually wear out their current interest and go on to something else. The point is, kids have to practice if they're going to be readers, and a few detours to meet Nancy and the gang are not going to interfere with their progress.

Where are our children going to get good books to read on a steady basis? From us, teachers and parents, so that one day they will be discerning readers. Yet so many educators and parents say to me, "I just don't have time to read to my kids. There's so much else to do." Well, let me tell you that that's a real cop out. You will always find time for what you believe in. When we say we don't have time because there are more important things to do, we are exposing our lack of knowledge of the reading process. How can we not have time for the love and joy of reading? How can we not have time to read to our kids, when it could so easily be the most important and enjoyable thing we do all day? How can we not have time to give our kids a solid lasting gift such as a lifetime of reading pleasure?

We are so caught up in giving rewards for reading a book. I think it's really getting out of hand. We have gone far beyond giving a grade or even a star, and I question both. We're now into ice cream, candy, and even pizza. How sad. Please keep in mind that the real reward is in the reading of the book, that wonderful feeling of being a part of the story, the feeling you get of not wanting the book to end, the feeling of knowing you have grown and changed in your thinking because of reading a particular book, being moved to tears or laughter as you follow interesting characters through their world. The rewards go on and on, and the flavors far surpass ice cream and pizza. The candy and ice cream might help some kids to get started, but with most it won't last. The empty calories for the body will be just as empty in nourishment for the mind.

In fairness to the business people who are genuinely trying to make a contribution to the education of the young, they can't be held totally responsible for this less than desirable approach to reading, for they have not been schooled in the elements of reading success. However, we, as educators, should know better. Remember what we're really after is, "Mr. Halloran, I loved this book. Have you got another good one?" or, "Mr. Halloran, I wrote a poem last night. Do you want to read it?" The real reward is in the reading of the book or the writing of a poem.

Fads in Education

It's interesting to watch the ongoing parade of fads that teachers get involved with. Every couple of years something new will sweep through the education community, and everyone, in fear of being left behind, jumps on the band wagon. Wave after wave keeps coming and with it such dedicated followers. I'm continually amazed at how each new fad is looked upon as the best, the ultimate, the end all. Whether it involves a new idea or a new piece of material, it is going to revolutionize the learning process.

Do you remember the overhead projector craze? Every classroom had to have an overhead projector, or it wasn't considered up to date and well-equipped. The problem with the overhead was that for many teachers it was the answer to a secret prayer. Now all they had to do was sit at that overhead and flash lessons on a screen all day. It was like a glorified workbook. And the unfortunate thing about it was that many administrators encouraged the constant use of the projector because of the huge financial investment that had been made. It was like part of a political platform. "In my school there is an overhead projector in every room." I'd rather have gone back to a chicken in every pot. A chicken in the hands of a poor cook could never do as much damage to the appetites of diners as an overhead in the hands of a poor teacher could do to the attitudes of kids. Looking back, I think the overhead projector was one of the worst fads to ever sweep the educational world, not in and of itself, but because of the way it was misused. We must have lost thousands of kids to boredom during that period.

Now we have thousands of overheads sitting in closets all over the country collecting dust. I wish there were a way to recycle them so that we could make book covers from them before someone decides to resurrect them under a new name. If we wait long enough the overhead projector will return. The sad part is that the overhead has quite a bit of potential. A man named Tom Concanon from New York did wonderful creative things with it. *Early Years Magazine* printed an excellent article of his suggesting interesting and creative uses of this teaching aid, proving that in the hands of a creative teacher it, like any other teaching aid, can encourage learning, rather than produce disinterested students. Beware, the overhead projector will be back.

Then, all of a sudden, we were catapulted into the open classroom. We tore down walls, built new schools without the usual number of inner walls, and forced two or more teachers to teach together in the same room or teaching space, as it was called. Before the first month of school was over there were new walls in place of the old. We learned to pile boxes and place moveable chalkboards into position to serve as dividers. Again, except in the hands of the few teachers who used the best teaching skills and common sense, had the support and help of their administrators, and enough time to research and plan implementation of a program suited to open space, we found ourselves with another disaster producing fad. There are still a few excellent open classrooms in existence being guided by intelligent thinking individuals who would probably be successful in any teaching situation.

Team teaching, which can be an excellent way to use the skills and talents of all teachers involved, was also foisted upon many good teachers who simply had incompatible personalities or teaching styles. The teachers who understood the concept and had like philosophies were, and still are, the successful ones. Unfortunately, many team situations ended in ruin. The race was on to see which building or system could boast a team teaching situation—all at the expense of the kids.

When are we going to learn that there are many valid teaching styles and techniques, but to implement a change successfully we must have time to study, understand, and plan thoroughly? When are we going to understand that if the classroom teacher does not accept the change, nor become invested in the change, the program is doomed before it begins? When are we going to recognize that the best teaching methods have been in use for centuries, and that they keep coming around with new titles? When are we going to understand that good teaching depends on cooperation between administrators, teachers, parents, and kids, equally if there is to be successful change and growth? When are we going to understand that the very best kind of learning takes place when the learner goes after knowledge for the sake of knowledge and not to comply with some new mandate?

You can always tell when a new wave is about to crash upon the shores of the educational world. All you have to do is watch the titles educational consultants use on their brochures. Often the title changes, but the presentation stays the same. I'm not entirely innocent of what I speak. Believe me, there were times when I wanted to change my brochure title to fit the current trend knowing it would bring me a lot of extra work. We tend to get so nervous about being left behind. Fortunately, I had the good sense to stick with children's literature and the love of reading, because it was the one thing I knew well and loved. I recognized that it fit everywhere. I didn't have to change to gifted education, or learning disabilities, or thinking skills, etc., because the literature fit all of the areas so naturally. It's strange how the literature will never be in the number one spot on the educational charts, and yet it is such an important area deserving of the attention of all educators. The most successful consultants, the ones with staying power, are the ones that remained in the fields-of education in which they were accomplished. They are the ones who learned to take the best of all other areas and apply it meaningfully.

Right now, children's literature is as close as it will ever get to being a fad. That pleases me because literature should never be the subject of a pendulum swing. But it is fun and funny to watch as people start to discover it, as if it were something new and wonderful. Wonderful, yes. But new? My hope is that we will come to realize that literature holds so much power by itself that it doesn't have to be rewarded with ice cream cones or stickers on charts. My hope is that, as an educational community, we will come to understand and appreciate the importance and the magic of literature, and that we will not have to ever be told to incorporate it into our curriculum, because it will already be the core, just as the library and the librarian should be the very center of the school. The next time you go into a school just notice where the library is situated and how well equipped it is—that is, if there is a library at all. We must learn to fight whomever, whether it be the school committee, the budget keepers, the administration, or our colleagues, to get the literature into the hands and minds of our kids on a daily basis. We must realize, once and for all, that literature is the heart of reading, and without the heartbeat the reading dies.

After the open classroom we quickly moved to special education and then on to gifted education. Then, with a loud and mighty roar, dawned the age of computers. I do believe computers will be in our lives from now on, but just about the time the ink was drying on the new brochures the wave was gone. That did surprise me, because of all the trends I thought this one would stay on the top of the list for a very long time, if not forever. I was wondering just how I could do a children's literature/computer workshop. It would be a get rich quick scheme if I could pull it off. Before I could work it out computers were already taking a back seat.

You might be asking, "To what did computers take a back seat?" Well, I don't know what we've been doing all these years but we had better stop and do some "critical thinking." That's the new term—the new money maker. Of course we can learn new and better ways to use our minds more efficiently, but my question is—why haven't we been using the best techniques for all of our teaching years? Surely formal education has been around long enough for someone to have pulled a solid thinking skills program together from kindergarten up. You must admit that it's something to think about, if you'll pardon the pun.

I'm sure you realize that we saw a few minor waves along with the major ones. "Make and take" really rode the crest of the wave for a while. Do you remember? We did everything from turning junk into teaching aids to building furniture out of cardboard. The cardboard furniture really helped many schools on a low budget. We happily made and took whole new classrooms! I know of only two people who did "make and take" language arts and math materials the right way, although I'm sure there were others. Jeanne Balawajder and Jean Healy knew their subject matter and taught the purpose and use of the materials before making them, so that they would not be used in isolation.

I remember flying three thousand miles to give a workshop, once. When I arrived I was told that the group was going to be making-and-taking while I talked. I think that was the saddest workshop of my career. All the time I was talking about the love of reading and how to pass the feeling on to our children, the whole group was cutting, pasting, sawing and painting. That was pretty early in my career, and I was taken by surprise by it all that I never said anything and went on with my talk. As I look back, I'm embarrassed for myself, for the school system, and for the teachers. Understandably, I have never forgotten that day. I learned a valuable lesson or two about honoring myself and about my responsibilities as an educator. I also had my eyes opened in regard to why other professions sometimes look down on us. In some instances, like the one I just mentioned, and there were others, can you blame them?

Then there was creative movement. I thought I was going to die during this period. We had to go to all those workshops, and we were told to wear our old clothes. Well, I knew what that meant. We were going to roll around on the floor for a few hours and make fools of ourselves. Even though creative movement has always been torture for me to the tune of hate, I do believe there should be a lot of it in classrooms.

I know that there are other teachers who feel as uneasy as I do about creative movement. Let me suggest that if you ever see a workshop presented by Lorraine Plum being advertised, do yourself a favor and go to her session. I think if we could all spend some time with Lorraine we wouldn't be afraid to promote movement in our classrooms. Lorraine is a master and has the amazing ability of making you think you are the only one in the room. You could be with a hundred other people, yet you would never feel you were being watched.

One of the difficulties with creative movement is that many of us are too self-conscious to do it. Another is that most of us don't think it's very important, not realizing how it can relieve stress, boredom, and fatigue. It actually promotes fun and self-awareness while tugging at the imagination.

For me, the pressure was on. Creative movement was in, and I was expected to get my kids involved. And I knew I had better get going. I'd soon be on the carpet if my plans did not reflect some movement. So I went looking for some books on movement. I always turn to the books when I'm in trouble. Sure enough, I found Rachael Carr's *Be a Frog, A Bird or a Tree.* I looked it over and thought, "I can do that." Then I found Mike Thaler's *How Far Will a Rubber Band Stretch?* I thought, "I can do that." Then I found Byrd Baylor's *Sometimes I Dance Mountains.* I didn't know about that one but I was willing to take a chance. I knew my kids would probably love all these books and all the lessons we could do from the books.

I went home, read my books, got my lessons ready and went into my classroom prepared to do creative movement. But every day I put off doing the lessons. Like most people, I hesitate when I'm not sure. Every day I'd go home and Phyllis, who of course was great at this movement stuff, would ask, "Did you do it today, Bill?" "I'll do it! I'll do it!" was my usual reply, followed by, "I'm waiting for just the right moment."

The right moment finally came. One day the sliding doors in my room flew open. There stood Stella asking me to take her class for about twenty minutes. I thought, "Why not do movement? It's now or never." And so I jumped into the world of creative movement with my head somewhere other than on my shoulders. I was ready—wasn't I?

I started out just fine. I said, "Okay, kids, please stand up and find your own space. We're going to do some-thing different today." We became birds, frogs, and trees, and we were great at it. We made our bodies into tiny rubber balls and then into huge rubber balls. We took an imaginary strong rubber band and put one end around our waists and the other end around the door knob, and we stretched our way down a long hallway. It was truly wonderful, and the kids were great. I was having so much success that I just couldn't stop. I didn't even realize that I was being drawn into a false sense of confidence. Why didn't I know?

I said, "Kids! Do you see that motorcycle next to you? Do you see that beautiful Harley Davidson?" I know, I know, I can hear you moaning now. But why didn't I know? I said, "Kids! Get on your Harley Davidsons and rev up your engines." They followed every direction eagerly. I didn't have to repeat one word. Have you ever heard sixty kids rev up their engines? The sound was deafening, but that was all part of this thing called movement, I reminded myself. I don't know what ever possessed me, but I heard myself saying, "Okay, kids, now GO!" I never saw anything like it in my whole life. Kids were everywhere. They were on the desks, under the desks, over the desks. They went up the walls and came down the walls with their engines going full force. I thought I was going to die. Suddenly the door opened and in walked Stella. You got it! She yelled—it was the only way she could be heard—"Bill, what the hell are you doing in here now?" I said, "Never mind that! Get these kids off the walls and help me get them back in their seats before we both get fired!" She said, "I see we're partners again."

The first thing the next morning, the kids asked, "Mr. Halloran, can we do that movement stuff again? It was wicked neat." Stella just gave me one look and I knew we wouldn't be doing movement in the fifth grade for a while.

In spite of my disaster, I really hope creative movement will find a lasting place in the classroom. I fear it won't, because it's difficult to get started and because many large waves have swept it back out to sea. This is one trend I believe would be of great benefit to kids and teachers. Maybe someday it won't be looked upon as a trend, rather as a necessary part of the curriculum from kindergarten through high school. The only system of which I am aware that does have it in its classrooms kindergarten through high school is in the area that produced the dancers I mentioned earlier who danced some of Eric Carle's books on his birthday.

There is one wave I'm waiting for, but I'm afraid I won't see it in my lifetime. I'm waiting for the era of the **magical teacher**—the dynamic teacher, the teacher who likes and understands kids, the teacher who loves the role of a teacher, the teacher who believes learning should be enjoyable no matter how difficult. Yes, I know there are many of you out there, but your magic wears a little thin when you're the only one in your school or your system. When we enter the age of the **magical teacher** we will have made progress, not just survived another fad.

Surviving

From the very first day of my teaching career I knew I'd have to find ways to survive as an educator. Even that first week I could never go right from my car to my classroom. I needed to ease into my day, so I quickly learned to take a detour from my car to the teacher's room. Car, teacher's room, classroom—I don't recall ever missing that route once in eight years. Even if I were an hour late for school—car, teacher's room, classroom. Some mornings Carl had to drag me screaming down the hall.

As the days, weeks and months passed I knew I'd have to find more ways to "ease in", to stay alive on a daily basis and arrive in my classroom. Eventually, I came to the realization that if I needed to ease in, the kids needed—no, deserved—the same consideration.

During my college years no one ever told me that my enthusiasm would be my finest teaching tool, and that that tool needed special attention and care. Why hadn't anyone warned me to guard my enthusiasm with my life? Why hadn't anyone made me realize that I would not survive without enthusiasm? Why hadn't someone explained that I could be overtly enthusiastic or quietly enthusiastic, but that I must be enthusiastic?

We, the teachers, set the pace in the classroom. If we are exciting, interesting, realistic, and enthusiastic, most of our kids will respond positively and discover their own enthusiasm. If we are dull, boring, unmotivated, and unenthusiastic, most of our kids will respond in like manner, and we will all die in our classrooms together.

In college I was told by some professors not to smile until January, because if I did I would lose control of my class. What nonsense! The worst part is that so many of us believed that destructive bit of advice. I didn't show my teeth until January, and by then, no one in my room even cared if I had teeth.

No matter how you feel, try to start your day on a happy note with a smile, a friendly gesture, a joke, a riddle, or a funny story. Don't be afraid to relax and fool with the kids for a few minutes to get the juices flowing. Laughter is a wonderful way to survive in the classroom, and if you take the time to really look and listen, there's always plenty to laugh about.

Often in some classrooms there doesn't' seem to be a time and place for warmth, fun, and laughter. I can't imagine teachers going out of their way to convince kids that learning shouldn't be fun, or interesting, or exciting. Most of the time we convince ourselves that we must be about the business of teaching. We are consumed with making sure our kids don't miss one isolated skill on some isolated list. Research has proved that anytime there is laughter, or simply the freedom to feel emotions openly in a classroom, learning will take place more readily. If the teaching is all factual and presented in a full emotionless manner, very little sustained learning will take place. Just problem solving alone is enhanced by the use of the imagination and the intuition, and there's nothing too factual in those areas.

Do you know how many teachers are found dead under their desks every year? Perhaps they are not physically dead, but they're dead for all educational purposes. I'm convinced that if we could keep joy and excitement in our teaching there would be fewer casualties. If we looked after ourselves and each other with care we would have a better track record. If we took on the responsibility of keeping teaching and learning a positive and comfortable experience the teacher/child estrangement rate would subside greatly.

Motivation is everything, and you have to work at it. It doesn't just happen. You have to search for it for yourself first, and then, when you have found it, hang on for dear life. Yes, teaching conditions are often poor, pay is usually ridiculous, and prestige is virtually nonexistent, but we must honor and respect ourselves if we are to be honored and respected by others.

The person who really understood motivation and about not giving up was the politician who lost his business in 1831, was defeated for the Legislature in 1832, failed again in a merchandising career in 1833, suffered an emotional breakdown in 1836, lost elections for speaker in 1838, elector in 1840, congress in 1843 and 1848, vice-president in 1856, but was finally elected president of the United States in 1860. Abraham Lincoln was motivated!

I guess I want to be like Lincoln. I want to persevere. I love being an educator, and I don't ever want to lose that love, joy, pride, excitement, and whatever you call that feeling that you get when you are doing what you were meant to do. I am aware, though, that it is so very difficult to hang on for twenty or thirty years, and it gets tougher every year.

I'm constantly looking for ways to hang in and hang on. Let me give you a few suggestions that worked for me when I was in the classroom.

1)   Get out of your classroom, mentally and emotionally. Enrich your own life by going to a concert, to a ball game, to a movie, to a lecture (not necessarily educational). Spend an evening with friends or a good book. Don't neglect yourself, your family or your friends. Some educators are notorious for spending every free minute on school related work, most of which turns out to be wasted energy. Remember, a

rich and full personal life will naturally flow into your classroom.

2)   Make sure you get a couple of breaks during the day. You need a breather from time to time. So many teachers tell me that their teacher's room is off limits except for the lunch or recess break. How sad! If that's the case in your school, hide in the boiler room or the broom closet for a few minutes. You need some quiet time, and I'm sure a colleague would understand and be happy to help look after the kids, especially if you're willing to do the same in return.

3)   Find a friend in the school. You need someone to share with, confide in, and to take your class for a few minutes whenever the need arises. There are times when you'll need a shoulder to cry on, or at least to lean on. Find someone you can trust, so you won't have to face the system or the world alone. And remember, too, that a triumph is sweeter, and a funny incident is all the more humorous when you have someone to share it with you.

I was lucky to have had three wonderful friends in my school. Ina and Stella, whom I have already mentioned in other parts of this book, and Ann Madsen. Ann had a way of keeping our school from being dull. She was, and still is, a doer—always involved, always in the middle of or causing the action, whatever it might be. We shared lots of laughs, joys, sorrows, and special memories. Mostly, I remember her as a wonderful teacher who was so very good to the kids. I think if it weren't for Ann, there would have been many days without joy or excitement. Our paths do not cross very often these days, but Ann will always remain a very important person in my memories of a very special time in my life. She was that school friend that we all need, the one who made it all bearable on the not so bearable days.

4)   Most of all, stay away from the negative people in your building and in your profession. They'll love destroying you and then leave you for dead before moving on to the next victim. These negative people are in almost every school in the country. They don't like the school, the curriculum, the administration, their colleagues, especially the successful ones, or even the kids. They're the way they are because they were never meant to be teachers in the first place. They're in the wrong slot, and they're taking it out on everyone who is willing to allow it to happen. Make sure you stay around the positive people, the ones who will be honest with you support you and work with you. These are the people who will help you to be the best you can be and to survive.

5)   Keep your lessons interesting. If you do this the kids will be excited about learning and about being part of that special world you are creating with them and for them. Of course, salt and pepper your lessons generously with children's literature. I know this is one of the best ways to stay motivated and alive. There is so much boredom waiting to happen, and the literature can do so much to help prevent it from ever getting a foothold.

I made up my mind a long time ago that no matter how difficult the going might get, I was going to spend my life as an educator. I'm proud to be a member of the education profession even in these hard times when there is so much criticism being leveled at us. I hold my head high in full knowledge that I am part of one of the most important professions in the world, and I hope you will join me in the celebration. It is time for educators to rejoice in the fact that we are playing a major role in shaping the future as we help children to shape their lives.

Rewards

In the beginning I thought the reward for teaching would be the paycheck. When I cashed my first check I knew there had to be something else. A nice fat check is certainly great, but there are other rewards. You just have to learn to recognize them at first. In fact, it will probably take a few years before the real rewards start coming along, but they do come. I was always taken by surprise by the time and place of coming upon the real gold in teaching. It usually came when I thought I couldn't go one more day, one more hour, one more minute in education. I'm sure you know the feeling. Just as you are telling yourself it's all over, you're leaving, that's it, finished—something happens. Someone slips you just enough gold to make you say to yourself, "I think I'll stay a little longer." Let me share some of my gold with you and perhaps you'll recall a few gold pieces of your own.

It was a Friday afternoon and the kids had all gone home. I was sitting alone at my desk trying to collect myself and muster enough energy to drag myself to the car. You do know what I'm describing here, don't you? All of a sudden the door opened, and there stood a kid I had had in class four years before. I knew that kid was going to spend the next forty-five minutes with me, and I was going to have to do most of the talking, because most kids that age don't carry on conversations with their past teachers. My heart sank because I wanted to leave, but before the forty minutes were over there was also great joy in my heart, because that boy came to thank me. He just couldn't put it into words. I stayed and talked, and in the end I walked to my car with new energy. A piece of gold was in my pocket, and in my head was the thought I was glad to be a teacher. I knew I'd hang in a little longer– at least one more day!!

I was sitting in an airport one evening when a man walked up to me and asked, "Are you Bill Halloran, the teacher?" I gave a weak yes for an answer, afraid I was going to have to talk education for the next three hours. He said, "I'm Mr. _____. You had my son Billy in the fifth grade." "Mr. _____," I replied, "I loved your son, Billy. He was a special kid and I'll never forget him. How is he? I can still picture him in my classroom." Mr. _____ grabbed my hand and squeezed it until I thought it would break. He said, "Thank you," and he was gone. I put another piece of gold in my pocket and thought, "I think I'll stay just a little longer."

There is something special to be found in every child. I wonder why I didn't know enough to search for the specialness in every child and say it right to the child? That should have been number one on my list of things to do as a teacher. I thought about it for a long time after hearing a very caring and sensitive man named Ray Wlodkowski speak about being with children. He knows that kids need to be reassured throughout their lives, that they are worthwhile and need to be respected. He knows that they can be so fragile and need our daily support. I wish I had heard him when I was an undergraduate student. I know I would have been the better for it, and my kids would have been the ones to profit most. These are things we should not have to learn on the job.

I see my friends Ina and Jerry Tober's son Craig a few times a year now that he's an adult and married. He's almost thirty, yet every time he sees me and someone is there whom I do not know, Craig always introduces me as "Mr. Halloran, my fifth-grade teacher." Craig gave me a pot of gold when he was in my class, and he still slips me a few extra pieces now and then. I have to tell you that in all honesty I love being introduced as his fifth grade teacher.

Then there was the time I was due to speak at the Howard Johnson's Motor Lodge in Orlando, Florida. The night before I was to give the speech I went to dinner with a couple and their young son who was in the fourth grade. I particularly remember how bright and alert the boy was. He joined in the conversation with such ease. We were coming back from dinner and my young friend suddenly got very excited and started yelling, "Look up there! Look up there!" I thought a rocket was going up. I quickly looked up and, Oh, Lord, there it was. In bright blinking neon lights, high on the marquis over the Howard Johnson's Motor Lodge were the words, "WELCOME TO ORLANDO, BILL HALLORAN." I couldn't believe my eyes. I figured I had made it to the mountain top. There was nowhere else to go after being on the Howard Johnson's marquis. The little boy was excited and the big boy was excited, too. We all had a wonderful laugh.

Shortly after getting back to my room the phone rang. I thought, "Who could be calling me at this hour? I don't even know if Phyllis knows where I am." When I answered the phone a voice on the other end said, "This is Barry Snyder. Is this Mr. Halloran?" I answered, "Yes." There was a pause, and then the voice said, "It's Barry Snyder!" to which I replied, "I heard you." Then he said, "Don't you remember me? I was in your fifth grade." It was one of my kids. "Oh, my goodness, of course I remember you. I had you and your sister Beth, and when you were in my fifth grade your mother was in training to be a nurse," I rattled off. With great surprise and delight in his voice he said, "You really do remember."

Isn't it wonderful when something like that happens,

and it all comes rushing back—sometimes? I then asked Barry what he was doing on the phone. "Well, Mr. Halloran," he said, "I moved to Orlando and I'm a senior here at the Orlando High School. I was driving by the Howard Johnson's Motor Lodge and I saw your name in blinking lights. How come?" "I'm a star", I said. He said, "At Howard Johnson's?" I said, "You take anything you can get."

We laughed and talked for a while. Then, toward the end of his call he said, "Can I ask you something?" I said, "Shoot! The world is yours tonight." Then he really made me smile. "Are you still twenty-nine?" he asked with a little bit of caution and a lot of mischief in his voice. I always told the kids I was twenty-nine. I said, "Barry, I'm twenty-nine and holding—with all my might" He laughed a little and then he said, "Stay twenty-nine, Mr. Halloran." I hung up the receiver, slipped another piece of gold into my pocket, and decided to stay "just a little longer."

I must tell you one more thing about my Howard Johnson's stay. I went to Orlando with a copy of *Where the Sidewalk Ends* by Silverstein for my young dinner friend. Before we left for dinner we sat on the couch while I read many of the poems. We laughed and laughed, and I knew I had given the boy the right gift. Several weeks later his father called me and told me his son loved the book so much that he took it to school to share with his teacher and classmates. When he presented the book with great joy to his teacher, she said, in front of the whole class, "We don't have time for that kind of nonsense in this room." His father went on to tell me that the boy went home, put the book on the bookshelf in his room, and never touched it again.

One thing I have discovered through my travels is that teachers across the country share so many common experiences and feelings but usually see themselves, especially in the hard times, as alone. Who hasn't had a class or two or three that has caused you to decide to quit teaching? Who hasn't had a few kids along the way who behaved as though they had been brought up light years away from civilization? Who hasn't wanted to lock the kids in and go home at 9:00 o'clock some mornings? Who hasn't cried silently for the taunted child, the disabled child, or the abused child? Who hasn't' been warmed by the whispered words "I love you"? Who hasn't been overjoyed at a simple break-through by one of your students? Who hasn't felt pride at having brought a shy child out of his shell? Who hasn't felt ashamed and pleased when a parent con-fided that you were the only one who had ever been kind to his daughter? Who hasn't felt underpaid and overworked? Who hasn't considered himself fortunate to be able to touch the lives of kids in a lasting way? It goes on and on, and yet there is probably no one situation that can be cited by any teacher on the East Coast that hasn't been experienced by some teacher on the West Coast. So, in view of this I am trying to pass on a few of my unique experiences that will have some of the same elements as your own experiences.

I think I should tell you about the old man and the little boy. I received a call from an organization on the West Coast asking me if I would speak to a group at a Saturday night P.T.O. meeting. I said, "What nut is going to give up a Saturday night on the town to go to a P.T.O. meeting?" The voice on the other end of the phone said, "We hope you will!"

I agreed to accept the invitation, but I certainly had misgivings. To my surprise, hundreds of people turned out. I asked the superintendent how he got all the people to come to the meeting. "Easy." he said, "We just told everyone that a man was coming here who could make their kids read." He looked at me for a moment and then walked away. "Well, don't do me any favors!", I thought. In all my life I had never been charged with a task so simply and directly. Of course, I wanted to succeed in the worst way, yet I knew it would be an impossible task to tell parents in such a short time how to turn their kids on to reading. It was as if I should have had magic dust in my pocket to sprinkle on the kids to make them read, for there would be no other method, to my knowledge, that would do the job.

I'll never forget the elderly man with a very young boy, about eight or nine, who sat in the row in front of me. For two hours while I spoke, they just stared at me, never changing their expressions. They made me uncomfortable, and I can't tell you why exactly. They just did. I even moved away from them as much as possible, but it didn't work. Their eyes went with me.

At the end of my talk the old gentleman moved toward me. I knew he wanted to talk with me. I avoided him for a time, but he was determined. Thinking I should get it over with, I went to him and asked if he wanted to talk about something. He said, "Mr. Halloran, that's my grandson with me. I want to know if you can help him. The teachers and administrators say he's slow. They say he's retarded, and I want him to read. I want to leave him that gift. How can I go about it?" I sensed the deep concern of this man for his grandson, and I recognized his sincerity. I asked him what he had been doing to help him up to this point. He said that he had been reading to the child every day. When I asked him if the boy liked being read to, he replied with a sparkle in his eye, "He loves it. It's his favorite time of the day."

I knew the boy had stared at me for two hours straight, but had he grasped any of what I was saying? I went over to the child and asked him if he liked the books I showed and talked about. He quickly answered,

"Yes!" I invited him to go to the table and pick out his favorites. He went right down my tables of books and picked about fifteen books, then came back to me clutching the stack. I commented that if he loved all of those books that I'd have to get some of them for him. He then surprised me when he said, "I want these books. I want to take these books now." Panic set in. I had the urge to grab them away. No, no. I'm just kidding. But they were my books!! I looked at the old man and said, "Just keep reading to him, and you'll give your gift." He smiled, thanked me and walked away with his grandson. This old man was a teacher, and he hadn't known it until that evening. You see, this boy who had been carelessly labeled retarded because his learning style didn't fit the teaching style of his teachers was able to do what most of the adults there that evening would probably have trouble doing. He listened for over two hours, knew which books he liked, and knew exactly where each one was located. Teachers come in many guises. It was worth traveling three thousand miles to meet this genuine teacher and his fortunate student. My pot of gold grew a little that night.

I have been very lucky collecting pieces of gold over the years. There have been so many wonderful, unforgettable rewards most of which came at such strange times and in such strange places like Howard Johnson's in Florida, airports, restaurants, etc.

One of my finest and most memorable rewards came from the town of Longview in the state of Washington. Ten years ago I went to Portland, Oregon to give a speech, and I showed the book *Peter's Pocket* by Judi Barrett. I had a teacher in the audience that day who loved the book. She went back to her school the next day and did *Peter's Pocket* with a group of first graders. In that group was a little boy named Monty. Monty was so taken with the idea of a pocket shirt that he went home and asked his mother to make him a Peter's Pocket shirt. His wonderful mother made the shirt immediately. That's some mother!

The next day when Monty wore his pocket shirt to school and walked up and down the halls, the idea of the pocket shirt snowballed; the whole school did pictures, stories, pockets and then sent me a gift. I'm sure you know what they sent me. That's right. I now have my own Peter's Pocket shirt. The only difference between mine and Monty's is that mine is extra large —and it fits! When I put my hand in one of the pockets there was a bright red lollipop in it.

It took me over a year to get to meet Monty. It was a very exciting time for me, as I'm sure it was for him. The meeting was so special that it is indelibly marked in my mind.

Ten years have slipped by since that moment in time, and I still have my shirt. I suspect that Monty still has his shirt, too. Most likely we will never meet again, but it doesn't really matter. The important thing is that a little boy and a man shared a memorable experience because of a book and a very special mother.

Let me tell you about one more reward that I received a year ago at Christmas time. It came from a girl named Louise. Louise was in my first class in 1966. Her father was dead, and she was letting me take his place. I knew that. We all know when something like that happens, or we should. I had my three reading groups, which were mandatory. Four little kids were in my "vulture group." I loved my vultures. The group consisted of three boys and Louise. I remember doing everything I knew how to do to get Louise to read. One day I even made fudge with my vultures because the story we were reading was about fudge. I must have spent two hours making the damn fudge with the kids, so they would enjoy reading the story just a little bit more. When we were finished, Louise ate the fudge and wouldn't read the story, of course!

I must add here that I was the only male teacher in the building, and I was told never to touch the children or to let the children touch me. If I did touch a child, I would risk losing my job. It was my first year, and I certainly didn't want to lose my job. How sad, when you stop to think of it. So many kids need a touch from the teacher once in a while. It just says to the kid, "Don't worry, I'm here, and I'll help you."

One day I was on the playground because I had the dreaded duty. Louise ran up to me with all the love and gusto only a child can have; she threw her arms around me. I quickly stepped back and said, "Louise, don't ever touch me." She just stared at me for a moment and ran. I have regretted not hugging her for the last twenty years. Fortunately for me, at the end of the twenty years I got a second chance.

It was the week before Christmas in 1986. I was going to have a meeting with Ina Tober. We decided to meet in Springfield which was between her home and mine. We went into a small restaurant that I had never been in before and sat down. The waitress came over and said, "Hi, Mr. Halloran. I'm Louise. Do you remember me?" Oh, my. Do I ever remember you," I said. "Do you still like fudge?" I inquired. She laughed and then asked me if I remembered reading *Charlie and the Chocolate Factory* to the class. I assured her I remembered. Then she told me that she was reading that same book to her nephew, and that he was loving it as much as she had loved it back in my class. It just reaffirmed for me the belief that the love of reading can be passed from one generation to the next so easily and painlessly.

As I got up to leave the restaurant that day, I went over to Louise, put my arms around her and said,

"Merry Christmas, Louise." I know we were both thinking of the same thing—that day on the playground.
Walking out the door, I thought, "How very wonderful
it is to be a teacher. I'm never going to leave."

Part Five
Looking Ahead

A Celebration

Phyllis and I have been down many roads together, professionally. We supported each other's careers, went on the road with our philosophy and ideas, and built our reputation in the field of literature and reading. The ten years we spent with the Learning Institute were excellent years, years of giving, taking, learning, and growing. It's interesting how, without much discussion at all, we both knew almost simultaneously that it was time to go down a new and very important road, yet, with luck, not our last road.

It was time for Phyllis to have time to write and publish her poetry, time for me to write this book, time for the two of us to share our book collection with as many teachers and kids as possible, time to gather together all the talented educators we had met over the years, time for exciting and meaningful programs for teachers, and time to bring a renewal of spirit—a joyfulness, and enthusiasm to our profession.

It's time for us to enter the period of the "magical teacher" and hope that it will not be a fad or just another pendulum swing. I truly hope that Phyllis and I will be able to spend the last phase of our careers helping to ensure that every child has that "magical teacher" every year. We are going to put continued energy into bringing to children and educators the love and joy of reading, wrapped in a sense of pride.

When we decided to head down this independent road we knew we were going to have to take the biggest risk of our lives. Although we had always been self-employed as consultants, we had always given a big chunk of our time and efforts to the Learning Institute. Now we were going to leave the security of the Institute. We were going to go out on our own and form our own company. After thoughtful and careful consideration, we decided to join forces with Don and Linda Sass, two people who care deeply about children and education. Don and Linda were already involved in a literature program for kids and teachers in the Northwest, the kind of program that had a natural connection to our work. Together we formed a company called Reading, Inc.

Reading, Inc., is dedicated to bringing to educators the best possible programs to aid them in their daily lives, as they guide children of all ages and abilities. We will present philosophical ideas as well as theories, techniques, methods, and materials for their consideration. We will never retreat from trying to instill or reinforce, wherever necessary, a sense of professional honor and pride in the teachers of this country.

I went to New York City to the Sheraton Hotel for seven days to think and to write this book, and I was able to write most of it by locking myself in a room or sitting in the lobby for ten or twelve hours a day. As often happens to professional writers, which I am not, I couldn't end my book. I searched and searched my mind but I couldn't come up with the right ending. Weeks and months passed, and I still couldn't get the ending right for the book. I wondered if I would ever find the right words. I really had hit a brick wall.

Then sitting in another Sheraton Hotel in Portland, Oregon, I suddenly realized, "I've got it!" I think there must be something about the Sheraton chain that helps me to write. Sorry, Holiday Inn.

In a way, the ending came to me by chance. Like many important moments in my life, it happened accidentally. Two people have continually put pressure on me to write a book. Phyllis and Don Sass, each for different but important reasons, have never given up on me.

"Write the book, Bill," became their campaign cry. Now, I can finish what they started.

I was driving to the Oregon coast with Don, and he was at me over the book. To put him off I said, "The book is done, but I don't have an ending." He was quiet for a moment and then told me how when he reads a book he always wonders why the author chose the title, and if he finishes the book and still doesn't know, he feels as though something is missing. I thought, "Of course, that's it. The title—why did I choose that title and what does it mean?" Spell it out, and the book will come full circle.

Being a teacher has always been so special to me. For a long time I thought I became a teacher when I received my college degree. How wrong I was. Over the years I've come to realize that degrees have very little to do with being a teacher. When you take the time to share, help, and care for your fellow man, you are a teacher. Age and degrees have little or nothing to do with it. Some of the finest teachers will never possess college degrees or even high school diplomas. Some of the most lasting lessons are taught by the very young and the very old.

Teaching is a celebration of giving and being given. It doesn't matter where or with whom the celebration takes place if there is honesty, trust and understanding present. We are all teachers in one way or another. Some of us teach very deliberately—all of us teach by example.

My formal teaching career was beginning, unbeknownst to me, as I sat in a hospital waiting room awaiting the birth of my son. Lord, I was excited. I was about to have a son, and his name would be David, my middle name. There was no room for debate over that. If Phyllis wanted another name, she was going to have to produce twins. The only other option would be divorce, and I would take the baby, David. Case closed!

I'll never forget how the doctor walked into the waiting room at 7:00 A.M. and said, "Mr. Halloran?" I said, "My son, is he here?" "Mr. Halloran," he repeated. "My son, is he here?" I repeated. Finally, he said, "Will you listen, please? Mr. Halloran, you have a beautiful daughter." "Oh, how wonderful," I said, "I always wanted a daughter!" I really was meant to have a daughter. It's quite wonderful the way things like that seem to work out.

When I first saw our beautiful baby she was all wrapped in a blanket, and Phyllis was holding her. All I could think of was the word "bundle." What a neat little bundle she was. When I took that little bundle into my arms I was so proud to be a father, not knowing that from that moment on I was going to be a full time teacher with no vacations and no coffee breaks. A celebration began that very exceptional day in a hospital room. Today, when I look at my lovely daughter, when I think of all the sons and daughters who spent a small part of their lives with me, and when I meet the educators across the country who take time to spend a few hours or days with me in the joint effort of trying to make life better for our kids, I can say, without reservation, that I am PROUD TO BE A TEACHER.

Like a seedling in spring
You trustingly gave me
Your youth,
That I might guide you
With the warming sunlight
Of my wisdom,
Refresh you
With the cooling showers
Of my laughter.

Like a thunderstorm in summer
You eagerly unleashed upon me
Your spirit,
That I might recognize
Your boundless potential
And give it nurture,
Your fiery courage
And remember mine
Now grown cold.

Like the turning leaves of autumn
You willingly allowed me
To see your inner self,
That I might know
your hopes, your fears
And not bring judgment,
Love you
In each of your colors
Without condition.

Like a snowflake in winter
You gently showed me
Your fragile uniqueness,
That I might find pleasure
In your every facet
With searching heart,
Forever value
Your intangible worth
With open mind

And through each season
And after
A voice calls out,
"I'm glad
That I did stay
A little longer.
You live in me,
I in you
And I am proud."

Phyllis Halloran